FINANCIAL POST

FPbonds
Government
2024

Grey House Publishing Canada
PUBLISHER: Leslie Mackenzie
GENERAL MANAGER: Bryon Moore

Grey House Publishing
EDITORIAL DIRECTOR: Stuart Paterson
MARKETING DIRECTOR: Jessica Moody

Grey House Publishing Canada
3 – 1500 Upper Middle Road
PO Box 76017
Oakville, ON L6M 3H5
866-433-4739
FAX 416-644-1904
www.greyhouse.ca
e-mail: info@greyhouse.ca

Grey House Publishing Canada Inc. is a wholly owned subsidiary of Grey House Publishing Inc. USA.

While every effort has been made to ensure the reliability of the information presented in this publication, Grey House Publishing Canada Inc. and Postmedia Network Inc. neither guarantees the accuracy of the data contained herein nor assumes any responsibility for errors, omissions or discrepancies.

Errors brought to the attention of the publisher and verified to the satisfaction of the publisher will be corrected in future editions.

Except by express prior written permission of the Copyright Proprietor no part of this work may be copied by any means of publication or communication now known or developed hereafter including, but not limited to, use in any compilation or other print or electronic publication, in any information storage and retrieval system, in any other electronic device, or in any visual or audio-visual device or product or internet product.

This publication is an original and creative work, copyrighted by Postmedia Network Inc. and Grey House Publishing Canada Inc. and is fully protected by all applicable copyright laws, as well as by laws covering misappropriation, trade secrets and unfair competition.

Grey House Publishing Canada Inc. has added value to the underlying factual material through one or more of the following efforts: unique and original selection; expression; arrangement; coordination; and classification.

Postmedia Network Inc. and Grey House Publishing Inc. will defend their rights in this publication.

© 2024, Postmedia Network Inc.
365 Bloor St. East
Toronto, ON M4W 3L4
Email: fpadvisor@postmedia.com
legacy-fpadvisor.financialpost.com

Text © 2024 by Postmedia Network Inc.
Texte © 2024 par Postmedia Network Inc.
Cover, Front Matter and Back Matter © 2024 by Grey House Publishing Canada Inc.
Couverture, matière première et publicités de produits © 2024 par Grey House Publishing Canada Inc.

Published in print form by Grey House Publishing Canada Inc. under exclusive license from Postmedia Network Inc. All rights reserved.
Publié sous forme imprimé par Grey House Publishing Canada Inc. sous licence exclusive de Postmedia Network Inc. Tous droits réservés.

Printed in Canada by Marquis Book Printing Inc.

ISSN: 1486-7273
ISBN: 978-1-63700-934-5

Cataloguing in Publication Data is available from Libraries and Archives Canada.

Contents

BANK OF CANADA ANNUAL REPORT 2023 vii
   Excerpts from the Bank of Canada's annual report for 2023, detailing topics such as monetary policy, the financial system, funds management, and the Bank's handling of high inflation.

CENTRAL BANK CRISIS INTERVENTIONS: A REVIEW OF THE RECENT LITERATURE ON POTENTIAL COSTS xliii
   A Bank of Canada report on how central bank interventions, which maintain the liquidity of high-quality assets, can create strong benefits for financial systems.

INTRODUCTION 1
   Description of the contents of the book.

PROVINCIAL UNDERWRITERS 2
   List of underwriting managers by province.

CANADIAN TAXATION 3
   Outline of the various tax levies in Canada that affect investments in debt obligations of or guaranteed by the Canadian Federal or Provincial Governments.

CANADA 9
   Statistical overview of the country.

DIRECT DEBT 10
   Table of Government of Canada direct debt, listed by maturity date.

GUARANTEED DEBT 11
   Table of Government of Canada guaranteed debt, listed alphabetically by government agency.

CALLABLE BONDS 14
   Table of Government of Canada callable bonds, listed alphabetically by government agency.

TREASURY BILLS 15
   Table of Treasury Bills, listed by maturity date.

ALBERTA 19
   Tables of direct and guaranteed debt following a statistical overview of the province.

BRITISH COLUMBIA 22
   Table of direct debt following a statistical overview of the province.

MANITOBA 25
   Table of direct debt following a statistical overview of the province.

NEW BRUNSWICK 28
   Tables of direct and guaranteed debt following a statistical overview of the province.

NEWFOUNDLAND AND LABRADOR 31
   Tables of direct and guaranteed debt following a statistical overview of the province.

NOVA SCOTIA 34
   Tables of direct and guaranteed debt following a statistical overview of the province.

ONTARIO 36
   Tables of direct and guaranteed debt following a statistical overview of the province.

PRINCE EDWARD ISLAND 41
   Tables of direct and guaranteed debt following a statistical overview of the province.

QUÉBEC. 43
   Tables of direct debt, guaranteed debt, and callable bonds following a statistical overview of the province.

SASKATCHEWAN 49
   Table of direct debt following a statistical overview of the province.

EUROBONDS. 53
   Debt offered in the European market, listed alphabetically by government issuer.

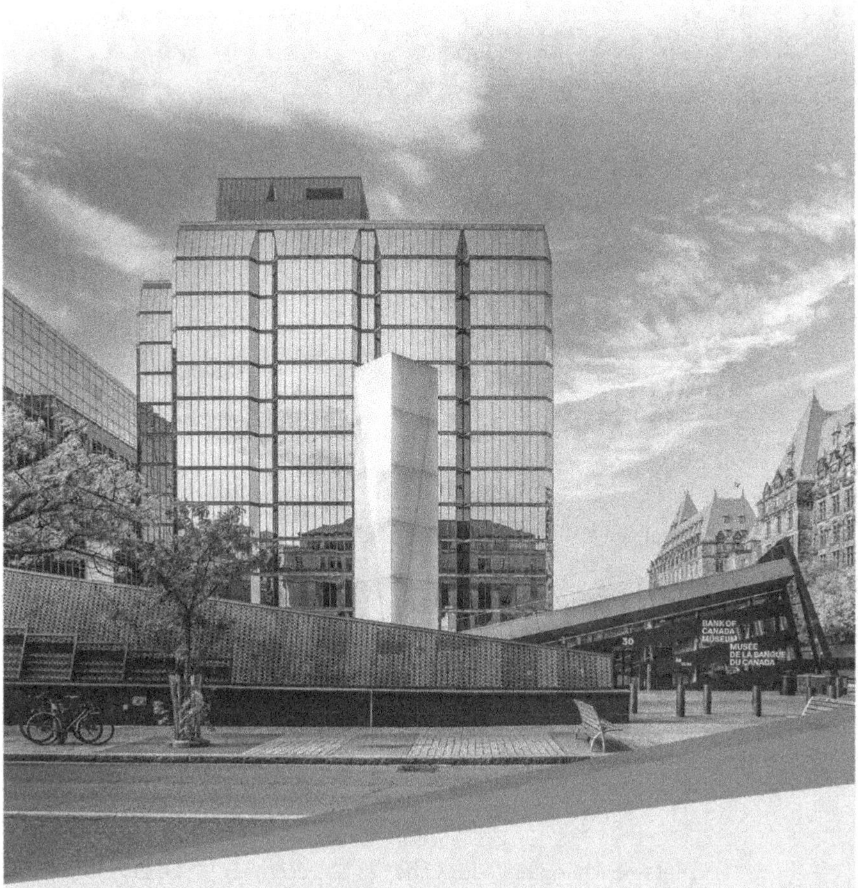

Annual Report 2023
DYNAMIC | ENGAGED | TRUSTED

2023 by the numbers

3.9%
Consumer price index inflation

5.00%
Policy interest rate at year-end

8
Number of Governing Council deliberation summaries published

$119.4
billion—Value of bank notes in circulation as at December 31, 2023

1.0%
Canada's average annual real gross domestic product growth as estimated at December 31, 2023

75.61
US cents—Exchange rate for Can$1 as at December 31, 2023

$179.8
billion—Nominal value of marketable bonds issued by the Government of Canada in 2023

$281.1
billion—Nominal value of Government of Canada bonds held by the Bank of Canada, a reduction of $88.4 billion since December 31, 2022

7
parts per million (ppm)—Counterfeiting rate in Canada as at December 31, 2023

89,423
Number of Canadians who participated in the Bank's public consultations on a Digital Canadian Dollar

2,350
Number of employees as at December 31, 2023

14
Consecutive years as one of Canada's Top 100 Employers

85
Percentage of employees who would recommend the Bank as a great place to work

Social media followers at year-end

2,570
Facebook

3,601
Instagram

250,050
X (formerly known as Twitter)

166,774
LinkedIn

Monetary policy

Canadian economic growth slowed significantly in 2023 as the effects of interest rate increases continued to work their way through the economy. Although inflation was still above the Bank of Canada's 2% inflation-control target at the end of the year, monetary policy tightening in Canada and abroad had slowed demand and started to ease price pressures.

Inflation in the consumer price index declined significantly from its June 2022 peak of 8.1% to reach 3.4% by the end of 2023. Despite substantial monetary policy tightening, progress toward the inflation-control target has been slower than anticipated.

The Bank raised its policy rate three times in 2023 for a total increase of 75 basis points. This brought the policy interest rate to 5% by July. From then on, Governing Council kept rates unchanged as it monitored signs that past rate increases were having the desired effects of bringing demand and supply into better balance and easing inflationary pressures.

https://youtu.be/iyqdnDBclOY

Monetary policy is one of the Bank's five main areas of responsibility. Learn more about the Bank's **core functions**.

The Bank used a variety of channels to communicate that it:

- would continue to assess whether the current policy interest rate would be sufficient to achieve the 2% inflation-control target
- was prepared to raise the policy interest rate further should inflationary pressures persist
- was carefully weighing the risks associated with both under- and over-tightening of monetary policy

Throughout 2023, the Bank continued its quantitative tightening (QT) as part of normalizing its balance sheet.

 Learn more about **inflation** and the Bank's **process for making monetary policy decisions**.

Monitoring inflation in the consumer price index

Over the course of 2023, evidence grew that the Bank's monetary policy was working. Inflation, which had been at 5.9% in January, fell to 2.8% by June. Although it briefly climbed back up to 4% in autumn, it eased to 3.4% by the end of the year. Despite this progress, inflation remained above the Bank's target throughout 2023.

Low energy prices drove much of the easing in inflation during the first half of 2023. Inflation in the prices of food and many other goods and services also showed signs of easing, as input costs decreased and demand began to slow. However, shelter price inflation remained high, mostly due to the rising costs of mortgage interest and rent. Overall, progress toward the Bank's inflation target was slower than expected.

Business and consumer expectations for near-term inflation also continued to ease in 2023, but they remained both higher than before the start of the COVID-19 pandemic and higher than the Bank's forecast for inflation. Bank survey results indicated that consumers and businesses expected inflation to be above the 2% target for the next two years. Expectations for longer-term inflation remained consistent with the 2% target. Results also revealed that businesses have continued to increase prices more than usual, indicating that corporate pricing behaviour has yet to normalize.

Key inflation indicators and the target range

Year-over-year percentage change, quarterly data

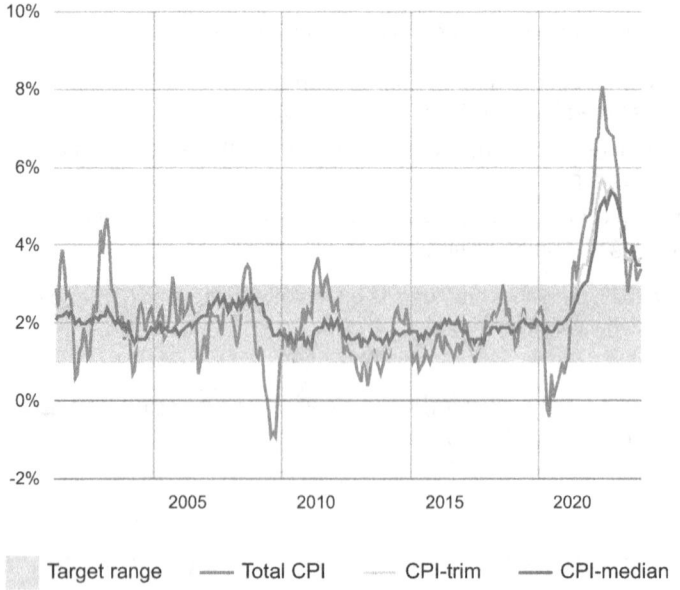

Implementing monetary policy and managing the Bank's balance sheet

The Bank, like many of its central bank peers, used a variety of tools to address high inflation and manage its balance sheet. These include increases to its policy interest rate and QT, which began in 2022 and continued through 2023. With QT, the Bank no longer replaces maturing Government of Canada bonds on its balance sheet. As a result, the size of the Bank's balance sheet continued to decline, from $410.7 billion at the end of 2022 to $316.8 billion at the end of 2023.

As well, the Bank began to assess its operational framework for implementing monetary policy and managing its balance sheet in anticipation of the new steady state. This work involved estimating the ultimate range and day-to-day management of settlement balances and offsetting assets, as well as reviewing the Bank's tools for market operations and asset acquisition.

This follows the Bank's 2022 **announcement** that it would implement monetary policy using a floor system—where the interest rate on the overnight deposit facility is equal to the target for the overnight rate. In 2023, the Bank further explained its rationale for maintaining this system.[1] It also provided some estimates for the steady-state range of settlement balances and the expected duration of QT.[2]

Learn more about **quantitative tightening** and the Bank's **balance sheet**.

https://twitter.com/bankofcanada/status/1704578744495599767

Rebalancing supply and demand

Gross domestic product grew solidly by 2.6% at the start of the year. However, economic growth stalled through the middle of 2023. The softening in demand was most visible in sectors that are sensitive to interest rates. For example:

- the housing market continued to slow
- consumer spending softened

- per capita consumption fell even though solid population growth continued to support overall spending

With slowing demand growth and rising supply, an increasing number of indicators suggested that the economy was in balance in the second half of the year.

Supporting the Bank's monetary policy function

Despite the highly complex forces affecting supply and demand, the Bank's forecasts correctly anticipated that in 2023:

- Canadian and global growth would slow
- inflation would fall significantly from the peaks observed in 2022

Achievement of target for consumer price index (CPI) inflation

Key indicators	Reference level	2017	2018	2019	2020	2021	2022	2023
CPI inflation (%)		1.6	2.3	1.9	0.7	3.4	6.8	3.9
Average CPI inflation since 2001 (%)	2.0							2.2
Inflation expectations at a 10-year horizon (%)	2.0	2.0	2.0	2.0	2.0	2.0	2.0	2.0

Analyzing inflationary pressures and the transmission of monetary policy

In 2023, the Bank continued its extensive analysis of inflationary pressures. As always, its macroeconomic models were essential in this work. Staff explored, among other topics:

- the supply side of the economy
- the role of structural changes in labour markets and immigration
- input costs and food prices
- supply-chain disruptions and near-shoring[3]
- the effects of pricing behaviour and markups on inflation[4, 5]
- the recent challenges faced by central banks in forecasting inflation[6]

Meanwhile, the Bank's consumer and business surveys continued to provide key information about Canadians' evolving expectations for inflation. As well, Bank staff engaged with outside experts on these topics.

The Bank also worked to better understand the effects of higher interest rates. It used its macroeconomic models, as well as detailed Canadian mortgage data, to capture the implications for mortgage interest costs and consumer spending. As well, it enhanced and updated its framework for assessing the health of the Canadian labour market and used microdata to better understand labour market dynamics.[7, 8]

Inflation dynamics in the rest of the world have been similar to those observed in Canada. Drawing lessons from a range of countries' experiences, the Bank analyzed the roles that monetary policy, inflation expectations and easing supply constraints play in the process of global disinflation.

Integrating a variety of data points to strengthen analysis

Given the high level of economic uncertainty during 2023, the Bank actively sought out new data and information sources to strengthen its analysis. These efforts included:

- enhancing the Bank's business and consumer surveys and making use of insights from its **Market Participants Survey**, the results of which were published for the first time in February 2023 following a successful pilot
- applying innovative approaches to non-traditional data, such as using textual analysis of news reports to track layoffs in real time and aggregating firm-level job postings to monitor vacancies by industry
- reviewing market intelligence practices to ensure the Bank is maximizing its engagement with stakeholders in financial markets
- exploring how valuation ratios in the Canadian stock market can help reveal investors' expectations about future economic growth
- developing a new analytical model that combines macroeconomic and financial market variables to estimate probabilities of various growth and inflation outcomes

Bank staff also explored research and data related to Indigenous economies in Canada and continued to examine how monetary policy affects them.[9] Such analysis gives the Bank a clearer picture of the different ways its actions affect various groups.

Assessing the implications of structural changes to the economy

Staff continue to investigate what structural changes mean to the economy—both in Canada and around the world. Research and analysis on their implications provide another input into the Bank's decision-making and monetary policy actions.

In 2023, this work included a variety of research on the implications of the surge in population that began in 2022.[10] Staff also explored the roles that digitalization, automation and the adoption of advanced technologies play in the Canadian economy. Notably, staff examined the implications of digitalization for labour markets, productivity, prices and monetary policy.

Learn more about the Bank's 2023 work on digitalization.

The effects of climate change are also an important driver of structural change. The Bank continued to integrate climate considerations into its research and analysis. This included developing an enhanced and expanded set of modelling tools for assessing the effects of climate change and the transition to a low-carbon economy. The Bank integrated the impact of green investment tax credits into its projection of business investment. In addition, staff analyzed the adverse effects of climate disruptions on international trade.[11]

Looking forward

In 2024, the Bank will continue to assess how higher interest rates affect inflation and the broader economy. In addition, the Bank will:

- adapt its balance sheet management and market operations to support the anticipated steady state
- continue to improve its macroeconomic models, including the ongoing development of a new suite of models to produce more accurate projections and better enable a risk management approach to monetary policy
- deepen its understanding of inflation drivers, including labour market tightness and wage developments
- enhance its surveys and outreach as well as the tools it uses to understand what structural changes mean for monetary policy and the economy
- publish its Indigenous Reconciliation Action Plan
- initiate a review of its COVID-19 pandemic response
- plan for the 2026 renewal of its monetary policy framework

More information

Monetary Policy Report

Framework for market operations and liquidity provision

Business Outlook Survey

Canadian Survey of Consumer Expectations

Market Participants Survey

The Economy, Plain and Simple

"Ending the pain of high inflation" (remarks by Governor Tiff Macklem)

"Understanding the unusual: How firms set prices during periods of high inflation" (remarks by Deputy Governor Nicolas Vincent)

"Rebalancing the economy while managing risks" (remarks by Deputy Governor Sharon Kozicki)

---

1. T. Gravelle, R. Morrow and J. Witmer, "Reviewing Canada's Monetary Policy Implementation System: Does the Evolving Environment Support Maintaining a Floor System?" Bank of Canada Staff Working Paper No. 2023-10 (May 2023).[←]

2. T. Gravelle, "The Bank of Canada's market liquidity programs: Lessons from a pandemic" (remarks to the National Bank Financial Services Conference, Montréal, Quebec, March 29, 2023).[←]

3. S. Kabaca and K. Tuzcuoglu, "Supply Drivers of US Inflation Since the COVID-19 Pandemic," Bank of Canada Staff Working Paper No. 2023-19 (March 2023); O. Kryvtsov, J. C. MacGee and L. Uzeda, "The 2021–22 Surge in Inflation," Bank of Canada Staff Discussion Paper No. 2023-3 (January 2023).[←]

4. R. Asghar, J. Fudurich and J. Voll, "Firms' inflation expectations and price-setting behaviour in Canada: Evidence from a business survey," Bank of Canada Staff Analytical Note No. 2023-3 (February 2023).[←]

5. P. Bouras, C. Bustamante, X. Guo and J. Short, "The contribution of firm profits to the recent rise in inflation," Bank of Canada Staff Analytical Note No. 2023-12 (August 2023).[←]

6. C. Conces Binder and R. Sekkel, "Central Bank Forecasting: A Survey," Bank of Canada Staff Working Paper No. 2023-18 (March 2023).[←]

7. S. Birinci, F. Karahan, Y. Mercan and K. See, "Labour Market Shocks and Monetary Policy," Bank of Canada Staff Working Paper No. 2023-52 (October 2023); S. Birinci, Y. Park, T. Pugh and K. See, "Uncovering the Differences Among Displaced Workers: Evidence from Canadian Job Separation Records," Bank of Canada Staff Working Paper No. 2023-55 (October 2023); L. Shao, F. Sohail and E. Yurdagul, "Labour Supply and Firm Size," Bank of Canada Staff Working Paper No. 2023-47 (August 2023).[←]

8. E. Ens, K. See and C. Luu, "Benchmarks for assessing labour market health: 2023 update," Bank of Canada Staff Analytical Note No. 2023-7 (May 2023).[←]

9. A. Chernoff and C. Cheung, "An Overview of the Indigenous Economy in Canada," Bank of Canada Staff Discussion Paper No. 2023-25 (October 2023).[←]

10. T. Gravelle, "Economic progress report: Immigration, housing and the outlook for inflation," (speech to the Windsor–Essex Regional Chamber of Commerce, Windsor, Ontario, December 7, 2023).[←]

11. G. R. Dunbar, W. Steingress and B. Tomlin, "Climate Variability and International Trade," Bank of Canada Staff Working Paper No. 2023-8 (January 2023).[←]

Financial system

The Bank of Canada plays an essential role in promoting and preserving the stability and efficiency of the Canadian financial system. This work helps to sustain economic growth and raise standards of living for Canadians.

In 2023, central banks continued to increase policy interest rates in response to high and persistent inflation. These elevated interest rates, while necessary to reduce inflation, tested the resilience of the global financial system.

In March, for example, banking sectors in the United States and Switzerland faced acute stresses. Authorities in those countries reacted swiftly to limit spillover effects. But these events underscored the need for financial system participants to adapt after more than a decade of low interest rates. These events also served as a reminder that risks can emerge and spread quickly, requiring increased vigilance from regulators and central banks.

 The financial system is one of the Bank's five main areas of responsibility. Learn more about the Bank's **core functions**.

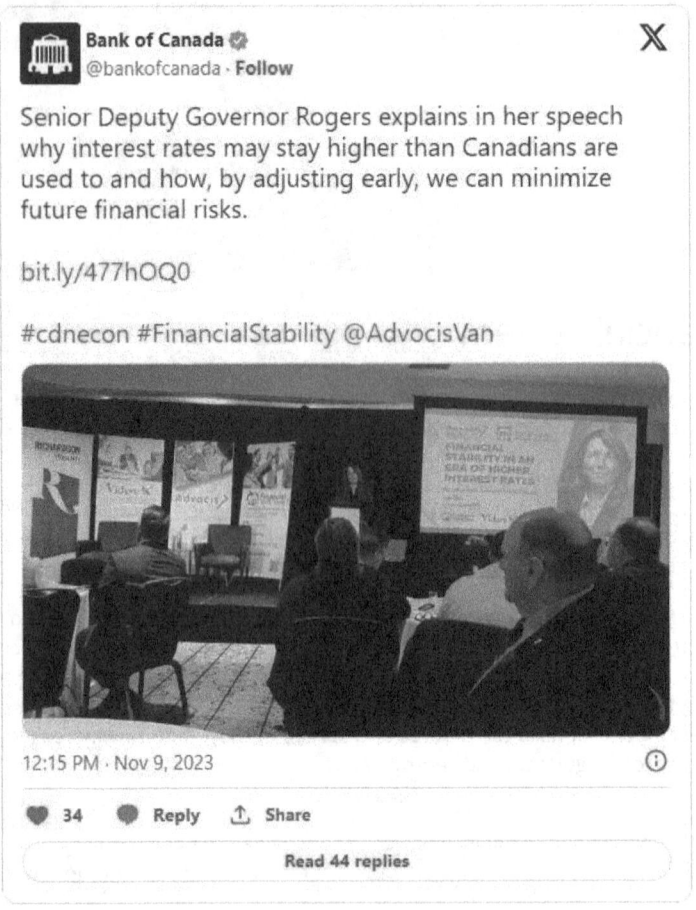

https://twitter.com/bankofcanada/status/1722664154631147861

Adjusting to higher interest rates and tightened financial conditions

Global financial conditions have tightened considerably because of monetary policy actions to reduce inflation. The strong response by central banks—including the Bank of Canada—helped to bring inflation down from its June 2022 peak. But it also exposed weaknesses in the global financial system—notably, those inherent in business models relying heavily on both low interest rates and low volatility.

The stresses that appeared in the international banking sector in March 2023 brought these weaknesses to light. In Canada, however, the financial system proved resilient, partly because Canadian banks had only small direct exposures to the troubled American and Swiss institutions. Additionally, Canadian banks are held to the highest global regulatory standards and are subject to rigorous supervision.

Canadian banks—like those around the world—are generally more resilient today than they were before the 2008–09 global financial crisis. Financial institutions have made significant improvements in their financial buffers and risk management practices. Regulators, too, have taken important steps to ensure the Canadian financial system remains robust. However, if global financial stress re-emerges and becomes persistent, the stability of the Canadian financial system could face challenges.

Supporting the Bank's financial system function

The Bank conducts rigorous research and analysis to inform its efforts to foster a stable and efficient financial system. It also collaborates with federal, provincial and international authorities as well as with industry.

Assessing vulnerabilities and risks

The 2023 *Financial System Review* (FSR) presented the Bank's assessment of key vulnerabilities and risks to the financial system. Its theme in 2023 was the adjustment to large increases in interest rates. Throughout the year, the Bank continued to leverage microdata to track how this adjustment was playing out for households and the financial sector. The Bank's key **indicators of financial vulnerabilities** suggested that early signs of financial stress had emerged.

https://www.youtube.com/watch?v=OPRcwXLCB3g

From a historical perspective, acute financial stress among Canadian households remained low in 2023. However, a severe recession could affect the ability of households to pay their mortgages, potentially leading to credit losses for lenders.

Additionally, the Bank analyzed the balance sheets of banks and non-bank financial institutions. Staff found that, although these institutions managed well in 2023, risks remain—notably to the cost and availability of funding.

As outlined in the FSR, the Bank continued to track other vulnerabilities and risks, such as those posed by climate change and digitalization. Staff published research and analysis on:

- the financing sources of Canadian organizations that report greenhouse gas emissions
- flood risks and their impact on lending for residential real estate
- climate transition risks and how they affect the financial system
- decentralized finance

Visit the Bank's **Financial System Hub** for more information about its work in these areas.

Analyzing the link between monetary policy and financial stability

The financial system plays an important role in transmitting monetary policy. In 2023, the Bank continued to assess how this transmission is occurring in the current interest rate environment. For instance, microdata on mortgage payments helped the Bank understand how much of an effect higher interest rates have had —and are expected to have—on reducing borrowers' disposable income.[12]

Considering the implications of financial market activity

As financial markets evolve, the Bank systematically conducts analysis to understand how these developments can affect the Canadian financial system, including its stability. In 2023, Bank staff conducted a variety of work in this area.

For example, staff analyzed the March 2020 trading behaviour in the Government of Canada bond market, at the peak of market turbulence. They found that hedge funds can contribute to one-sided markets and amplify declines in market liquidity.

Another study of the behaviour of market participants found that Canadian life insurers did not face significant draws on liquidity during recent stress periods (such as the COVID-19 pandemic) and were able to maintain their usual investment activities. In contrast, other types of asset managers saw their liquidity needs increase significantly and therefore likely contributed to market stress during these periods.

Bank staff also found that options markets can provide a gauge of investor risk sentiment during times of stress. A review of the price movements of options on exchange-traded funds suggested that investors did not anticipate an adverse scenario for major Canadian banks or the economy during the global banking turmoil in March 2023.

These studies helped shed light on how different market participants respond during stress episodes.

Promoting financial system resilience

The Bank worked closely with federal and provincial authorities in 2023 to monitor and assess the resilience of Canada's financial system.

This collaboration included the Bank's continued leadership of the **Heads of Regulatory Agencies Committee** and the **Systemic Risk Surveillance Committee**. Through these federal–provincial forums, the Bank helped improve information sharing on important financial system topics.

The Bank continued to work with industry through the **Canadian Fixed-Income Forum** (CFIF). Efforts focused on promoting an efficient and robust market for fixed-income securities for Canada. The Bank also agreed to co-chair the **Collateral Infrastructure and Market Practices Advisory Group (CIMPA)**. This new industry working group will foster operational efficiency in the Canadian markets for securities financing and collateral. The group will also identify areas for potential improvement and implement and promote recommended solutions.

Ensuring a robust interest rate benchmark regime for Canada

The **Canadian Alternative Reference Rate Working Group** (CARR), which is co-chaired by the Bank, continued its work in 2023 to advance benchmark reform in Canada. It completed the first stage of its two-stage transition plan to move the market away from the Canadian Dollar Offered Rate (CDOR). As of the end of June, market participants had adopted pricing based on the Canadian Overnight Repo Rate Average (CORRA) for almost all new derivative and securities transactions.

To support the second stage of the plan—and since CDOR will no longer be published after June 2024—the Bank worked with CARR members to encourage the loan market to quickly adopt CORRA. The 2023 launch of CARR's forward-looking one- and three-month term CORRA benchmarks will help this stage of the transition.

In October, CFIF announced its proposed path for winding down the issuing of bankers' acceptances (BA). This path will ensure the Canadian money market continues to function well. In recent years, BAs have been the second-largest product in Canadian money markets after treasury bills; they will no longer be issued after CDOR disappears.

Overseeing payments and financial market infrastructures

The Bank is responsible for overseeing Canadian **financial market infrastructures** that have the potential to pose systemic or payment system risks. In October 2023, the Bank **designated** four payment systems as prominent under the *Payment Clearing and Settlement Act*:

- Visa Inc.'s VisaNet
- Mastercard International Inc.'s Global Clearing Management System
- Mastercard International Inc.'s Single Message System
- Interac Corp.'s Inter-Member Network

The designation of these systems brings them under formal Bank oversight and requires them to follow the Bank's risk management standards. This will help ensure the systems remain safe, viable and effective methods of payment for Canadians.

 Learn more about the Bank's regulatory oversight of prominent payment systems.

Looking forward

In 2024, the Bank will continue to:

- closely monitor how households, businesses and the financial system adjust to a higher interest rate environment
- use microdata to enrich its understanding of financial vulnerabilities and provide timely updates to Canadians on how these vulnerabilities are evolving
- work closely with domestic and international partners to share information and promote the resilience of Canada's financial system
- complete benchmark reform to help ensure Canadian markets function well by finalizing and supporting the smooth transition away from CDOR

More information

Financial System Hub

Financial system committees

Global Financial Stability Reports from the International Monetary Fund

---

12. See M. teNyenhuis and A. Su, "The impact of higher interest rates on mortgage payments," Bank of Canada Staff Analytical Note No. 2023-19 (December 2023).[←]

Funds management

As the fiscal agent and banker for the Government of Canada, the Bank of Canada carried out a variety of activities in 2023. These included:

- administering the government's domestic cash balances
- conducting debt auctions and bond buyback operations
- managing the assets and liabilities of the Exchange Fund Account (EFA)

The Bank also provided banking, settlement and custodial services for other clients, such as financial market infrastructures and other central banks. At the same time, the Bank managed its own investments and liabilities as part of the ongoing normalization of its balance sheet.

 Funds management is one of the Bank's five main areas of responsibility. Learn more about the Bank's **core functions**.

The value of domestic Government of Canada bonds issued in 2023 was $179.8 billion. The total stock of domestic marketable debt was projected to reach $1,390 billion by the end of the 2023–24 fiscal year.

Chart 1: Gross bond issuance by tenor

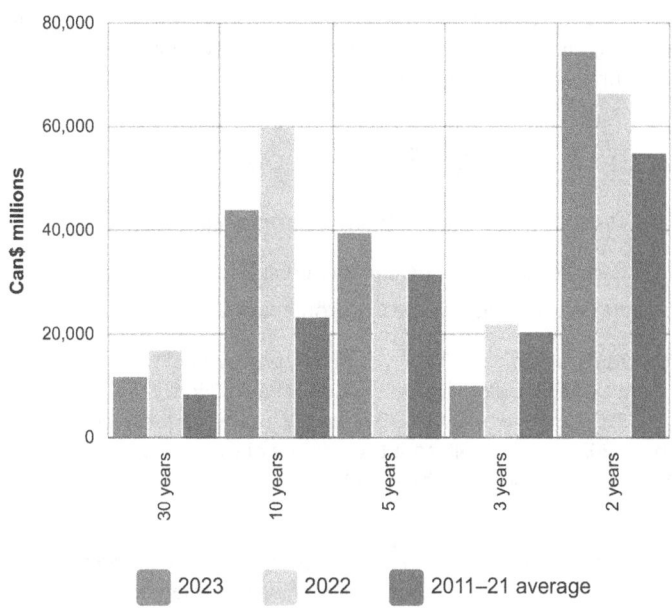

2023   2022   2011–21 average

Supporting the Government of Canada's domestic funding and liquidity needs

Bank staff worked closely with the Department of Finance Canada and consulted with financial market participants to:

- raise stable and low-cost funding for federal programs and services
- maintain a liquid and well-functioning market for Government of Canada securities

Advising the Government of Canada on its debt issuance

The Bank provided advice to the Government of Canada on discontinuing the issuance of bonds in the three-year sector and reallocating bonds to other tenors. This advice was based on findings from staff research and feedback from financial market participants.

The Bank also updated the methodology it uses to set medium-term targets for outstanding debt across different tenors. This will help in assessing the costs and risks associated with the government's debt strategy.

Reviewing Canada's prudential liquidity plan

The Bank contributed to a review of the Government of Canada's prudential liquidity plan by analyzing various sources of liquidity. The Bank assesses the plan every five years to ensure the government can satisfy its payment obligations if normal access to funding markets is temporarily disrupted.

Managing the Exchange Fund Account

The Government of Canada's reserves of foreign currency are held in the EFA to:

- promote orderly conditions in the Canadian-dollar foreign exchange market
- provide a source of liquidity for the Government of Canada

During the 2022–23 fiscal year, the Bank managed the growth of the EFA to about US$82 billion from US$75.5 billion, an increase of US$6.5 billion. Over the remainder of 2023, the Bank worked to grow the EFA to the target value of US$87.5 billion for 2023–24. Overall, about two-thirds of the reserves were invested in US-dollar assets, with the balance held in euros, British pounds sterling and Japanese yen.

The Bank also raised funds through short-term US-dollar securities and medium-term cross-currency swaps. These involved exchanging Canadian dollars for foreign currency to acquire liquid reserves.

In April, the Bank led the issuance of a five-year US$4 billion global bond, which was the largest issue size ever from Canada in foreign currency. Demand for the bond was very strong, as evidenced by:

- the large number of orders
- the quality of investors
- the tightening of pricing during execution

Managing Canada's reserves in a world of reduced liquidity

The Bank also started to evaluate and improve liquidity in the EFA to guard against potential crises. This work has become increasingly necessary since the start of the COVID-19 pandemic because general market liquidity has declined—including liquidity from US government securities—while global macroeconomic and financial uncertainty remain elevated. This has prompted global reserve managers like the Bank to increase their focus on maintaining enough liquidity in their portfolios. Such liquidity may be required to intervene directly in foreign exchange markets to counter disruptive movements.

Modernizing collateral management

In 2023, the Bank implemented the first release of a system that will enable seamless, flexible and resilient management of collateral through the full trade cycle—from initiation to settlement to reporting. This was a key milestone in the redesign of the technologies and processes that support the Bank's domestic market operations and Canada's payment systems.

The new system will improve:

- the efficiency and robustness of the Bank's repurchase and securities lending operations
- the Bank's ability to adjust or introduce liquidity operations in response to market stress

 Learn more about the Bank's market operations, programs and facilities.

Repatriating retail debt operations

In 2023, the Bank repatriated operations for the Government of Canada's Retail Debt Program. The Bank now services and redeems the government's outstanding retail debt—roughly $452 million in Canada Savings Bonds and Canada Premium Bonds. These operations had been outsourced since 2001.

Looking forward

In 2024, the Bank will continue to:

- provide advice to the federal government on managing debt, reserves and liquidity
- build on technology and process improvements that support the Bank's domestic market operations and Canada's payment systems

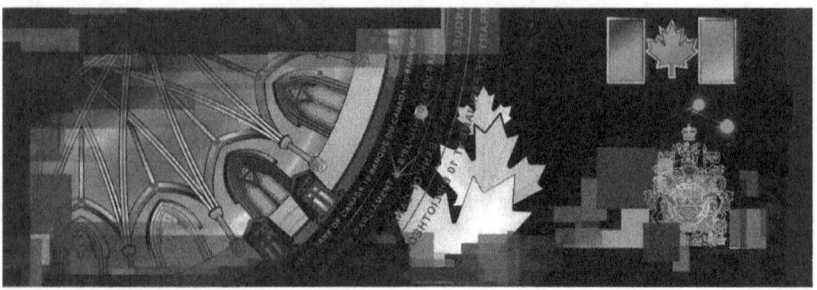

Currency

In 2023, the Bank of Canada continued to:

- provide Canadians with secure bank notes
- monitor the payment preferences of Canadians
- research the future of cash

The Bank also conducted research to better understand and reduce the environmental impacts caused by producing and distributing bank notes. At the same time, the Bank began work on a new design for the $20 bank note, and staff continued to explore the possibility of a Digital Canadian Dollar.

 Currency is one of the Bank's five main areas of responsibility. Learn more about the Bank's **core functions**.

Meeting the demand for cash with bank notes Canadians can trust

The Bank continued to supply financial institutions with bank notes to meet the demand for cash. Roughly 3 billion bank notes were in **circulation** in 2023.

Surveying Canadians about cash use

The Bank regularly surveys consumers and businesses to better understand how and why they use cash. This information helps the Bank assess Canadians' awareness of, attitudes toward and behaviours around bank notes.

The results of the Bank's 2022 Methods-of-Payment Survey show that many Canadians still use cash and that 80% of consumers have no plans to go cashless.

Meanwhile, cash acceptance remains almost universal across businesses in Canada. Results from the 2023 Merchant Acceptance Survey reveal that 96% of small and medium-sized businesses accept cash.

The Bank conducts the Bank Note Confidence Survey twice a year to assess public confidence in the authenticity of bank notes. In 2023, roughly 96% of Canadians expressed confidence that the bank notes they use are real. This aligns with a **low counterfeiting rate** of 7 parts per million (ppm)—well below the Bank's benchmark of 30 ppm.

Canada's bank notes, including the vertical $10 note featuring Viola Desmond, highlight Canadian achievements around the country, around the world and even in space.

Informing decisions through research

The Bank conducted research to better understand:

- the use, availability and acceptance of cash in Canada as well as trends in payment preferences
- changes in the regulatory landscape for national and international cash systems
- the ownership of digital currencies and cryptoassets in Canada as well as the implications of fintech innovations for financial stability
- the policy, economic and technical implications of a Digital Canadian Dollar, including its potential effects on private banks
- the latest innovations in bank note security features to guard against counterfeiting

- options to make the life cycle of a bank note more environmentally sustainable

Exploring a Digital Canadian Dollar

Through policy, economic and technical research, the Bank continued to explore the possibility of a digital form of the Canadian dollar. This potential form of money would:

- be issued by the Bank
- provide benefits similar to those provided by cash—in other words, it would be:
  - safe
  - universally accessible
  - private

As part of its ongoing consultation on a potential Digital Canadian Dollar, the Bank invited Canadians to participate in a survey to share their views and perspectives. The survey focused on what features would matter most to Canadians if Parliament and the Government of Canada were to decide that a digital form of the Canadian dollar is needed. The consultation generated almost 90,000 responses.

In November, the Bank published a report summarizing key takeaways from its outreach activities on this topic over the past two years.

https://youtu.be/h9ZeIXrCiDs

Read the Bank's consultation summary report.

Designing the next $20 bank note

On May 6, 2023, the day of King Charles III's coronation, the Office of the Prime Minister of Canada **announced** that a portrait of His Majesty would be featured on Canada's next $20 bank note. The Bank initiated the design process for the new note, which will feature a significant step up in security, have a vertical design and be made of polymer.

Greening Canada's bank notes

The Bank launched a project to identify opportunities for reducing greenhouse gas emissions, water consumption and waste from producing, distributing and recycling bank notes. This work aligns with the Bank's **climate change strategy** as well as with the **Government of Canada's plan to reduce greenhouse gas emissions**.

Looking forward

In 2024, the Bank will continue to:

- research the use, availability and acceptance of cash in Canada as well as trends in payment preferences
- investigate trends and changes in the regulatory landscape for national and international cash systems
- engage with financial institutions, the broader cash industry and others who play a role in cash system infrastructure to prepare for the future of cash
- conduct policy research and analysis to inform planning for any future Digital Canadian Dollar, including technical design work and monitoring of the payments landscape
- work on the next $20 bank note

More information

Methods-of-Payment Survey

Merchant Acceptance Survey

Bank Note Confidence Survey

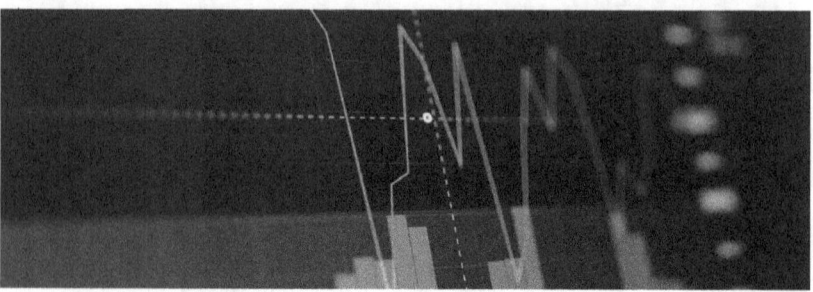

Financial results

Overview

This section provides the key highlights of the Bank of Canada's financial results for the year ended December 31, 2023. These highlights should be read with the financial statements and accompanying notes for the year ended December 31, 2023. Management is responsible for the information presented in the Annual Report.

Since the onset of the COVID-19 pandemic, the Bank has used extraordinary measures to restore the proper functioning of financial markets and support the economic recovery. In response to high inflation following the reopening of the Canadian economy, the Bank rapidly raised its policy rate and undertook quantitative tightening, in which maturing bond holdings are not being replaced. Refer to the Bank's **website** for more information on these measures, including the relevant **press releases** and **market notices**.

Managing the balance sheet

Financial position
(in millions of Canadian dollars)

As at December 31	2023	2022
Assets		
Loans and receivables	6	5
Investments	292,341	378,206
Derivatives—indemnity agreements with the Government of Canada	23,406	31,346
All other assets*	1,023	1,153
Total assets	**316,776**	**410,710**
Liabilities and deficiency		
Bank notes in circulation	119,430	119,726
Deposits	196,212	273,333
Securities sold under repurchase agreements	6,638	17,396
Other liabilities	342	352
Deficiency	(5,846)	(97)
Total liabilities and deficiency	**316,776**	**410,710**

* All other assets includes Cash and foreign deposits, Capital assets and Other assets.

The Bank's holdings of financial assets stem from its unique role as the exclusive issuer of Canadian bank notes and its activities related to monetary policy and the financial system. The value of the assets on the Bank's balance sheet has declined due to the Bank's quantitative tightening measures, as a result of improved market conditions and economic performance. The Bank's total assets decreased by 23% during the year to $316,776 million as at December 31, 2023. The main driver of this decrease was the maturity of investments.

Investments decreased by 23% to $292,341 million as at December 31, 2023. This decrease was driven mainly by the following movements within the Bank's holdings:

- Government of Canada securities, which include nominal bonds and real return bonds, decreased by $72,051 million during 2023. This decline is mainly due to the bonds maturing. This resulted in a decline of $47,914 million in Government of Canada bonds held at fair value and a decline of $24,137 million in Government of Canada bonds held at amortized cost.

- The Bank engages in repo operations, which provide market participants with a temporary source of Government of Canada securities on an overnight basis. These operations also improve the availability of the Bank's holdings of Government of Canada securities. The volume of **securities repo operations** declined during 2023, resulting in a decrease of $11,759 million in securities lent or sold under repurchase agreements, compared with December 31, 2022.

Derivatives—indemnity agreements with the Government of Canada refers to the indemnity agreements that were put in place to indemnify the Bank and allow it to support Government of Canada, provincial and corporate bond markets. Losses resulting from the sale of assets within the Government of Canada Bond Purchase Program, the Provincial Bond Purchase Program and the Corporate Bond Purchase Program are indemnified by the Government of Canada, whereas gains on disposal are remitted to the government. The $23,406 million balance represents the fair value of the derivatives associated with the net unrealized losses on these assets as at December 31, 2023. Derivatives decreased by $7,940 million during the year, mainly due to a slight decline in long-term bond yields. This is represented in the asset profile chart by "All other assets."

Asset profile

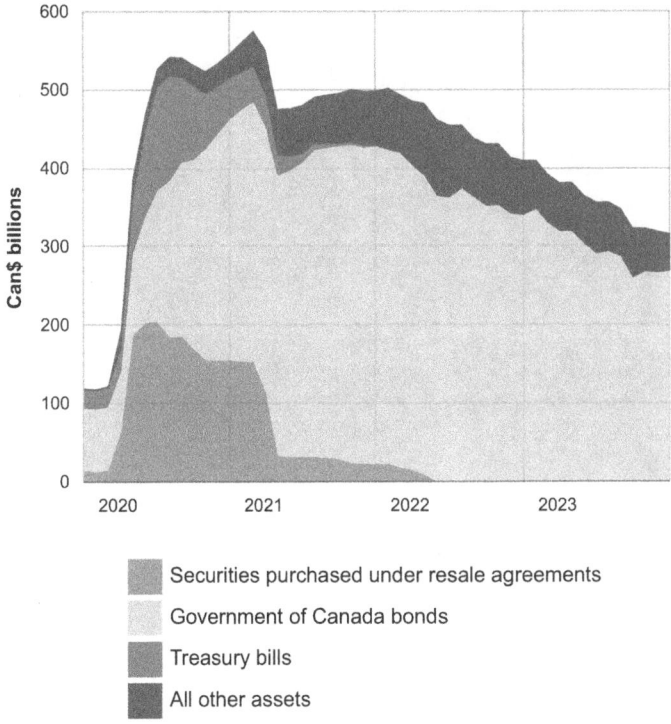

- Securities purchased under resale agreements
- Government of Canada bonds
- Treasury bills
- All other assets

Bank notes in circulation represents approximately 37% (29% as at December 31, 2022) of the Bank's total liabilities. The number of bank notes in circulation remained almost unchanged from their level on December 31, 2022.

Deposits consists of deposits made by the Government of Canada, members of Payments Canada and others. This balance has declined by 28% to $196,212 million as at December 31, 2023, compared with December 31, 2022, reflecting continued quantitative tightening.

Securities sold under repurchase agreements decreased by 62% to $6,638 million as at December 31, 2023, compared with December 31, 2022. This liability represents the repurchase price for **securities repo operations** and **overnight reverse repo operations**. The Securities Repo Operations program supports core funding markets and the proper functioning of the Government of Canada securities market. Overnight reverse repos help to effectively implement monetary policy by withdrawing intraday liquidity, complementing the standing deposit and lending facilities.

Liability profile

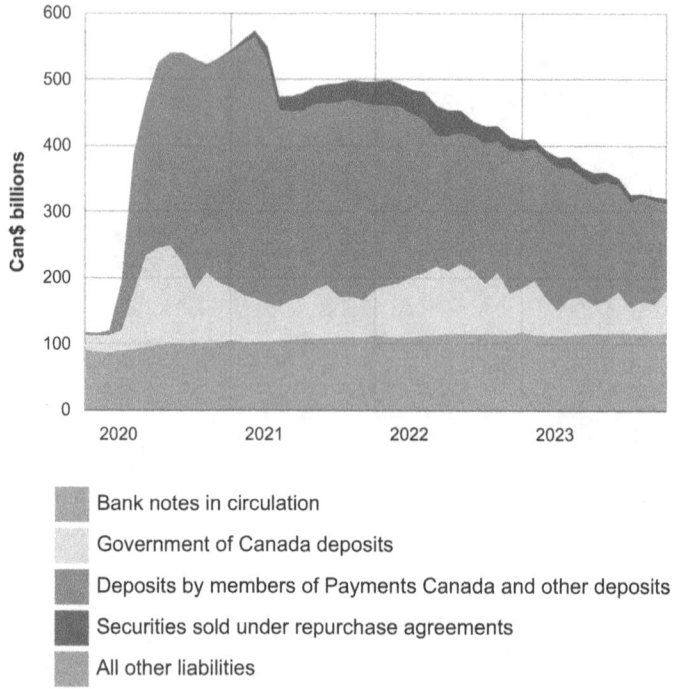

- Bank notes in circulation
- Government of Canada deposits
- Deposits by members of Payments Canada and other deposits
- Securities sold under repurchase agreements
- All other liabilities

Deficiency increased to $5,846 million as at December 31, 2023, as a result of net losses of $5,652 million for the year. As at December 31, 2023, the accumulated deficit was $6,738 million. *Deficiency* also includes the following offsetting amounts: $5 million of authorized share capital, a special reserve of $100 million, an investment revaluation reserve of $463 million and an actuarial gains reserve of $324 million, each as at December 31, 2023. Refer to Note 14 in the financial statements for more information about the Bank's deficiency.

Results of operations

Results of operations
(in millions of Canadian dollars)

For the year ended December 31	2023	2022
Interest revenue	3,850	4,373
Interest expense	(8,826)	(4,786)
Net interest expense	**(4,976)**	**(413)**
Other revenue	14	14
Total loss before operating expenses	**(4,962)**	**(399)**
Total operating expenses	(690)	(712)
Net loss	**(5,652)**	**(1,111)**
Other comprehensive income (loss)	(97)	406
Comprehensive loss	**(5,749)**	**(705)**

The Bank incurred a net loss of $5,652 million for the year, primarily because the interest expense incurred on deposits was greater than the interest earned on investments. The interest expense on deposits was higher because the Bank increased its policy rate from 0.25% in the first quarter of 2022 to 5.00% in the third quarter of 2023. In time, the Bank will resume generating net income. The net losses do not affect the Bank's ability to carry out its mandate.

Interest revenue depends on market conditions, the impact of those conditions on the interest-bearing assets held on the Bank's balance sheet, and the volume and blend of these assets. The Bank earns interest on its investments in Government of Canada securities, on securities purchased under resale agreements (if any) and on assets acquired through large-scale asset purchase programs. In 2023, interest revenue decreased by $523 million (or 12%) compared with 2022. This decline was driven by the Bank's lower average holding of interest-yielding investments throughout the year, which was partially offset by a slight increase in the average yield on investments.

Interest expense consists mainly of interest incurred on deposits held by the Bank. During the year, the interest expense increased by $4,040 million (or 84%) compared with 2022, resulting from rises in the Bank's policy interest rate. The increase was partially offset by a lower average volume of deposits during the year and by a decrease to 0%, in effect since May 2022, in the interest paid on Government of Canada deposits.

Operating expenses in 2023 decreased by $22 million (or 3%) compared with 2022. This primarily reflects a decrease in costs for staff, offset by an increase in costs for technology, telecommunications and other operating expenses.

- *Staff costs* decreased by $38 million (or 10%) during the year, compared with 2022, as a result of the following changes:
    - Salary costs increased by $20 million (or 8%) because positions were filled to deliver the Bank's core functions, including the new function of retail payments supervision. The annual compensation adjustment also contributed to the increase.
    - Benefits and other staff costs decreased by $58 million (or 43%), mainly due to a decline in the expense associated with the Bank's defined-benefit plans. This decline was a result of a rise in the discount rates used for their calculation.[19]
- *Technology and telecommunications* costs increased by $7 million (or 7%) compared with 2022. This increase was driven by the Bank's focus on its digital transformation and on strengthening the resilience of its information technology systems.
- *Other operating expenses* increased by $9 million (13%) compared with 2022. This was driven primarily by an increase in expenses associated with strengthening cybersecurity and integrating digital applications, aimed at improving the Bank's resiliency.

Other comprehensive loss for the year was $97 million. It includes a remeasurement loss of $120 million on the Bank's defined-benefit plans as a result of a decrease in discount rates,[20] offset by an increase in the fair value of the plans' assets. It also includes a $23 million increase in the fair value of the Bank's investment in the Bank for International Settlements.

Looking ahead through 2024

The Bank's 2024 plan
(in millions of Canadian dollars)

	2023 budget		2023 actuals		2024 budget	
For the year ended December 31	$	%	$	%	$	%
Staff costs	419	52	340	49	379	54
Bank note research, production and processing	60	7	52	8	13	2
Premises costs	35	4	36	5	34	5
Technology and telecommunications	118	15	111	16	122	17
Depreciation and amortization	78	10	73	11	74	10
Other operating expenses	96	12	78	11	85	12
Total operating expenses	**806**	**100**	**690**	**100**	**707**	**100**

The year 2024 represents the last year of the Bank's 2022–24 strategic plan, *Delivering on Our Promise*. The Bank's financial management framework enables decisions about allocating resources to achieve the Bank's objectives and mitigate risks in a prudent fiscal manner.[21]

Staff costs continues to represent the largest portion of the Bank's expenditures, while production costs for bank notes are expected to decrease due to existing reserves. Other expenditures include the cost of enhancing systems and tools to support operations, sustain the Bank's resilience posture and prepare for the future. These costs also contribute to fulfilling the Bank's new core functions, advancing its digital transformation and mitigating risks. In 2023, the Bank did not spend its full budget, mainly due to lower-than-planned staff benefit costs resulting from a change in the discount rates and the timing of other operating expenses.

Accounting and control matters

For details of the Bank's financial reporting framework and accounting matters, refer to the annual *financial statements*.

Internal control over financial reporting

The Bank maintains a framework to evaluate the design and effectiveness of internal controls over financial reporting. This framework includes disclosure controls and procedures to provide reasonable assurance about the reliability of financial reporting and the preparation of the financial statements in accordance with International Financial Reporting Standards. Every year, the Bank certifies its internal controls over financial reporting. This process is based on the Internal Control–Integrated Framework issued by the Committee of Sponsoring Organizations of the Treadway Commission and on the Control Objectives for Information and Related Technologies framework.

---

19. Benefit costs for a given period are based on the discount rate as at December 31 of the preceding year (e.g., the rate at December 31, 2022, was used to calculate the benefit expenses for 2023). Discount rates and related benefit costs share an inverse relationship: as rates decrease, benefit expenses increase (and vice versa). The discount rates used to calculate the pension benefit plans and other benefit plan expenses ranged from 2.6% to 3.1% for 2022 and from 5.0% to 5.1% for 2023. This increase resulted in decreased benefit costs for 2023.[↵]

20. The net defined-benefit liabilities are measured using the discount rate in effect as at the period-end. The rate applicable to the net defined-benefit liabilities as at December 31, 2023, was 4.6% (a range of 5.0% to 5.1% as at December 31, 2022). See Note 12 in the financial statements for more information.[↵]

21. The Bank's forecasts for its operations do not include projections of net income and financial position. Such projections would require assumptions about interest rates, which could be interpreted as a signal of future monetary policy.[↵]

Reproduced with the permission of the Bank of Canada, 2024.

BANK OF CANADA
BANQUE DU CANADA

Staff Discussion Paper/Document d'analyse du personnel—2023-30

Last updated: December 11, 2023

Central Bank Crisis Interventions: A Review of the Recent Literature on Potential Costs

Patrick Aldridge, David A. Cimon and Rishi Vala

Financial Markets Department
Bank of Canada
paldridge@bankofcanada.ca, dcimon@bankofcanada.ca, rvala@bankofcanada.ca

Bank of Canada staff discussion papers are completed staff research studies on a wide variety of subjects relevant to central bank policy, produced independently from the Bank's Governing Council. This research may support or challenge prevailing policy orthodoxy. Therefore, the views expressed in this paper are solely those of the authors and may differ from official Bank of Canada views. No responsibility for them should be attributed to the Bank.

DOI: https://doi.org/10.34989/sdp-2023-30 | ISSN 1914-0568 ©2023 Bank of Canada

1 Introduction

Central bank interventions in a financial crisis can be effective at both maintaining market functioning and implementing unconventional monetary policy. Lending programs by central banks can ensure solvent market participants are able to access liquidity in exchange for good collateral, one of the original recommendations from Bagehot (1873). Asset purchases can both guarantee the liquidity of relevant assets and serve as a key unconventional monetary policy tool. Bernanke (2022) argues that, in the latter case, quantitative easing (QE) can add between 3 and 4 percentage points to the central bank's effective lower bound for interest rates.

Liquid government bond markets are key to well-functioning financial systems. A high level of liquidity in these markets can ensure participants are confident in their ability to access liquidity in exchange for high-quality assets. In turn, there is a lower probability of asset fire sales and contagion between financial institutions. The ability to avoid these negative outcomes means that central bank interventions, which maintain the liquidity of high-quality assets, can create strong benefits for the financial systems.

Despite these benefits, large-scale actions such as asset purchases and lending facilities at central banks are bound to have side effects and unintended consequences. An analysis of central bank interventions requires a proper accounting of not only the benefits but also these costs. Even among central bankers these large-scale asset purchases and lending facilities remain somewhat controversial. A 2017 survey of central bank governors showed a plurality of respondents (38.2%) deemed that it was "too early to judge" whether QE using government debt should remain in central bank tool kits after the 2008–09 global financial crisis (GFC), while 20.6% responded that it should be discontinued (Blinder et al. 2017). An evaluation of costs poses two difficulties: costs may be difficult to measure, and the line between intended and unintended consequences from central bank facilities may be unclear. Despite these limitations, a growing academic literature addresses the unintended consequences and side effects of central bank crisis actions. In our paper, we review this literature.

We focus on two major forms of central bank actions: large-scale asset purchases and large-scale lending facilities. Other central bank activities, such as conventional monetary policy actions, forward guidance or regulatory actions, are outside the scope of this review. We focus on the costs and side effects of these facilities to the financial system, rather than addressing all possible outcomes; for example, we do not address broader macroeconomic costs or accounting issues.

In our literature review we highlight papers that propose mechanisms by which central bank actions may create costs or side effects as well as papers that document the existence and magnitudes of those same effects.[1] We categorize financial system costs into four groups, which the existing literature has provided evidence in favour of:

- impacts on market and funding liquidity (section 2)

- pricing distortions (section 3)

- conflicts between monetary policy and financial stability objectives (section 4)

- rent-seeking and other unproductive uses of central bank liquidity (section 5)

Finally, we discuss actions central banks have taken to mitigate the costs and side effects of their intervention programs (section 6). Table 1 in the appendix provides a summary of papers discussed in each section.

2 Impacts on market and funding liquidity

Central bank interventions, whether in terms of asset purchases or lending programs, are often intended to improve the liquidity of eligible assets during a crisis. A central bank

---

[1]For additional information, a more focused, policy-oriented review of these costs can be found in Logan and Bindseil (2019), while a high-level discussion of these costs is presented in Bernanke (2022).

provides an outlet, outside of private markets, for participants to either sell or borrow against their assets. By acting as a large and committed buyer, the central bank could increase liquidity provision by dealers, reduce their inventory risk, stimulate trading activity through portfolio rebalancing and reduce contagion effects from disorderly asset sales (Diamond and Rajan 2005; Bessembinder et al. 2016; Boneva et al. 2022). However, recent evidence suggests that the impact of these actions may not be unidirectional. For example, Boneva, Islami, and Schlepper (2021) differentiate between the short-term flow effects and long-term stock effects of central bank fixed-income purchases on market liquidity, suggesting that while interventions improve liquidity measures contemporaneously, long-term impacts may be quite different. As a central bank removes assets from the market during large-scale purchases, liquidity measures may deteriorate because fewer bonds are available in private markets. An alternative mechanism, proposed by Boermans and Keshkov (2018), suggests that central bank asset purchases tend to attract price-elastic investors who in turn sell their bonds to the central bank. This exit of price-elastic investors then leads to an increase in the concentration of bond holdings among price-inelastic investors, hampering future liquidity by reducing the quantity of bonds available for trade. In a similar vein, Ferdinandusse, Freier, and Ristiniemi (2020) show that asset purchases are effective at initially improving liquidity, but as scarcity is induced and yields fall sufficiently to discourage new buying, liquidity begins to fall.

The work above suggests that market liquidity can be significantly affected by the underlying supply (float) of bonds available for market participants. The supply of bonds on the private market depends on the actions of both the fiscal and monetary authorities during a crisis. During the COVID-19 pandemic, many central banks purchased a large percentage of available government bonds. For example, the Bank of Canada (BoC) had $428 billion of Government of Canada (GoC) bonds on its balance sheet at its peak (January 2022), up from $80 billion in January 2019. At the same time, total bond issuance by the Government of Canada increased from $579 billion to $1.02 trillion. As a result, the BoC's holdings moved from 14% to 42% of all issued GoC bonds, as seen in Chart 1. Following October

Chart 1: The Bank of Canada's purchases of Government of Canada bonds during COVID-19

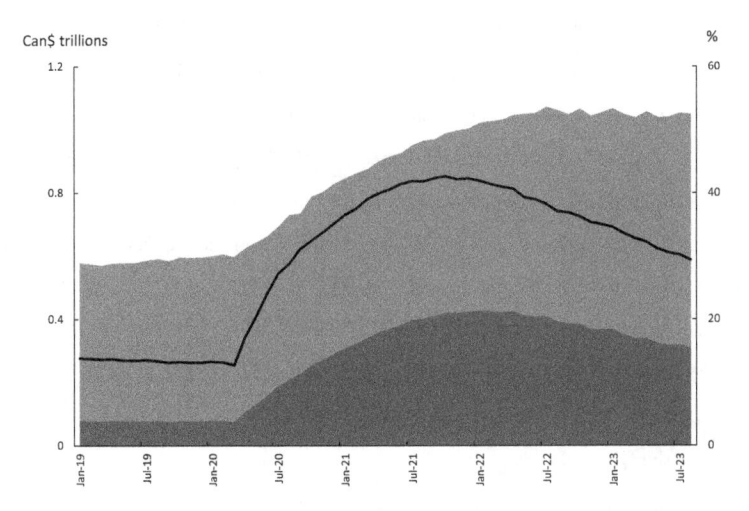

■ Bank of Canada's GoC bond holdings (left scale)   ■ GoC bond float in the market (left scale)   ▬ Percentage held by Bank of Canada (right scale)

Note: Chart 1 illustrates the Bank of Canada's holdings of Government of Canada (GoC) bonds, compared with the total float of those same bonds, during the COVID-19 period. The combination of Bank of Canada holdings of GoC bonds (red) and the GoC bond float (blue) is equal to total GoC bonds outstanding. GoC bonds include nominal and real return bonds. All amounts are in par values.
Source: Bank of Canada calculations Last observation: August 31, 2023

2021, the BoC's proportional holdings of GoC bonds began to fall as the GoC bond float began to increase, representing a reversal of this trend.

A straightforward signal that fewer bonds are available for trade following a central bank intervention is a decrease in either realized trading volumes or potential trading volumes through measures like market depth. Kurosaki et al. (2015) show that, following the Bank of Japan's (BoJ) quantitative and qualitative easing in the fall of 2014, the median volume of limit orders at the best-ask and best-bid price in the Japanese Government Bond futures market, a proxy for market depth, declined to 25% of its peak in mid-2014. Similarly, Schlepper et al. (2020) show that order book depth in interdealer markets fell by EUR1.3 million following a EUR100 million German government bond purchase by the European Central Bank (ECB) through its public sector purchase programme (PSPP).

Central bank asset purchases have gone beyond government bonds and, in turn, there may be additional costs from buying corporate bonds, mortgage-backed securities (MBS) or equities. Kandrac (2018) shows that an increase in the Federal Reserve's stock of MBS resulted in a deterioration of trade sizes and trading volumes and the total number of trades. Specifically, the average daily amount of MBS purchased by the Federal Reserve during the reinvestment phase of the MBS program reduced trade sizes, on average, by 7.6% from the previous day, and the average purchase amount during the Federal Reserve's third phase of QE (QE3) reduced trade sizes by 5.7% from the previous day. The impact on trading volumes was, on average, an increase of 2.6% during the reinvestment phase and a decline of 3.4% during the QE3 phase.

Another group of liquidity measures are those related to bid-ask spreads. Pelizzon et al. (2018) suggest that the impact of the BoJ's QE program may have a time component, with bid-ask spreads increasing as bonds became scarcer over the course of QE. Depending on the stage of the BoJ's QE program, bid-ask spreads for a given Japanese government bond increased between 0.33 and 1.5 basis points for a 1% increase in the share of the amount outstanding held by the BoJ. In the later stages of the BoJ's QE program, bid-ask spreads on a given bond changed by an additional -0.48 to 2.2 basis points for a 1% increase in the share of the amount outstanding of that bond's close substitutes held by the BoJ. Similarly, Abidi and Miquel-Flores (2018) suggest the bid-ask spreads of corporate bonds start to increase three weeks after the announcement of the ECB's corporate sector purchase programme (CSPP), increasing by 4.4 basis points in the third week and up to 17 basis points by the sixth week.

Another possibility is that asset purchase programs may increase bid-ask spreads only under specific circumstances, explaining why some studies, such as Kandrac (2018) and Schlepper et al. (2020), find mixed results. It is difficult for theory to provide a satisfactory explanation for why specific bond purchase thresholds by a central bank may create negative impacts. As a result, the literature has relied on ex-post analysis of different thresholds to explain the differential impacts of government purchases. Blix Grimaldi, Crosta, and Zhang (2021) find that, in the case of the Sveriges Riksbank, negative impacts on asset volatility were up to four times higher once they had purchased at least 40% of a particular bond's outstanding quantity. Han and Seneviratne (2018) show evidence that 40% of a bond's value outstanding being held by the BoJ corresponded to an increase in that bond's estimated bid-ask spread just above one standard deviation. Boneva et al. (2021) show that relative impacts of the ECB's German corporate bond purchases on bid-ask spreads were worse for older bonds compared with more recently issued ones, suggesting that older bonds with a lower free float were more negatively impacted.

Signs of market liquidity issues may be visible in lending markets (i.e., repo markets) rather than for outright fixed-income transactions (i.e., cash markets). A common measure of a bond's availability in the repo market is its "specialness," the difference between the general collateral repo rate and the repo rate for transactions using that specific bond. The logic of this measure is simple: if a bond is in scarce supply, borrowers who pledge this bond as collateral can borrow cash at lower rates. D'Amico, Fan, and Kitsul (2018) show that QE purchases by the Federal Reserve increase specialness of treasuries, and that this specialness lasts up to three months. They find that specialness increases not only for recently issued treasuries but also for seasoned treasuries. Specialness would increase by 1.84 basis points for the average purchase amount of recently issued treasuries by the Federal Reserve on the day of an operation and by 0.12 basis points for the average purchase size of seasoned treasuries. The impacts of QE on repo specialness translated to lower yields on treasuries relative to a fitted yield curve, demonstrating visible scarcity effects in both repo and cash markets for treasuries. Similarly, Arrata et al. (2020) show that the ECB's asset purchases increased specialness by 0.78 basis points for a purchase of 1% of the underlying bond's amount outstanding, while Corradin and Maddaloni (2020) show that this specialness was also associated with a 0.32% higher probability of failures to deliver.

Finally, given that repo markets are an important source of funding for market participants, many central banks implement some of their lending facilities through repo markets. A known issue with lending facilities is that those who access the facilities, often bank-owned dealers, are not always the ultimate demander of liquidity. These dealers are often intermediating liquidity through matched repo transactions to other market participants such as non-bank financial institutions (NBFI). Because these other participants typically do not have direct access to central bank facilities, dealers retain some market power in the transaction. Hüser (2021) shows that although aggregate repo spreads increased during the COVID-19 crisis, these increases differed sharply across NBFI sectors, which indicates that rates from emergency facilities are not fully passing on from dealers to NBFIs.

Dealers may be unable to pass through lending as a result of their own constraints. Exploiting a regulatory change in reporting requirements of the leverage ratio that affected only a subset of dealers, Kotidis and Van Horen (2018) compare repo activity between UK dealers affected by the regulatory change and thus more bound by the leverage ratio with the repo activity of unaffected UK dealers. They show that for a given client, repo volumes on average decreased by 66 percentage points, and the number of repo transactions declined by 39 percentage points among affected UK dealers relative to unaffected dealers.[2]

To explain movements in US Treasury yields and rates on repo transactions during the height of the COVID-19 crisis, He, Nagel, and Song (2022) show that dealers charge a spread on repo transactions over their own borrowing cost equal to their balance sheet cost. They find that repo spreads have increased by about 20 basis points around quarter-end dates,

---

[2]The 66% decrease in repo volume reflects a decrease in volume by affected UK dealers and an increase in repo volume by unaffected UK dealers.

when balance sheet constraints are known to bind more for European banks. Overall, they demonstrate how intermediary constraints can lead to higher costs for market participants seeking to engage in repo activity during crises, when dealer balance sheets tend to expand. Supporting the importance of balance sheet constraints, Breckenfelder and Hoerova (2023) find that, in response to ECB facilities, dealers with worse financial conditions during the COVID-19 crisis increased lending to investment-grade corporate bond mutual funds 1.4 to 1.6 times more than dealers with stronger financial conditions. The authors also highlight that the effectiveness of repo facilities at supporting mutual funds is capped by the regulatory limits on mutual funds' borrowing.

3 Pricing distortions

A second category of consequences from central bank interventions is changes in the pricing of securities. Often, central bank interventions are intended, at least to some degree, to modify the pricing of securities. During a financial crisis, this may be because market participants are engaging in fire-sale behaviour, artificially depressing the prices of otherwise safe assets below their fundamental values. In this case, interventions may be intended to return securities to their "fair" value. However, not all price changes caused by interventions are either intended or desirable. For example, interventions may distort long-term relationships between securities by lowering the yields of relatively riskier securities below those of safer counterparts.

Pasquariello (2018) argues that interventions may induce violations of the law of one price by complicating signals about the fundamental value of assets targeted by central banks. Similarly, Steeley (2015) argues that while the Bank of England's (BoE) QE program narrowed bid-ask spreads, it did so at the cost of creating return anomalies, thus reducing the efficiency of market prices. In particular, between the BoE's first and third phase of QE, gilt prices were slower to adjust to the arrival of new information, as shown by higher correlations between past and present gilt returns relative to their pre-QE levels. This autocorrelation could be exploited to generate excess returns (after accounting for transaction costs) during the during the period between the first and second phase of QE. Barbon and Gianinazzi (2019) argue that, in Japanese equity markets, the use of price-weighted instead of value-weighted baskets by the BoJ tilted its holdings in a manner that distorted the composition of aggregate systematic risk held by the private sector. This act distorted prices by generating abnormal returns around announcements for those stocks that experienced the greatest reduction in systematic risk as a result of the BoJ's purchases.

Price distortions may be seen through changes in the prices between otherwise similar assets and modifications of arbitrage relationships. Pelizzon, Subrahmanyam, and Tomio (2023) show that bond scarcity induced by ECB QE purchases increased transaction costs (bid-ask spreads) and the costs of borrowing securities (specialness), thereby distorting the arbitrage mechanism between futures and cash markets (a mechanism that we revisit when discussing monetary policy pass-through). Specifically, a 10% increase in the ECB's holdings of either German or Italian bonds widened the bid-ask spread of those bonds by 25% and increased their specialness to a level five times higher than it was before QE. This, in turn, corresponded to an increase of the cash-futures basis by 46 basis points, which started from a level of near zero before the commencement of the ECB's QE program.[3] Lucca and Wright (2022) show that, after the Reserve Bank of Australia's (RBA) yield targets under its yield curve control (YCC) program were no longer consistent with expectations of the monetary policy rate path, yields of targeted bonds decoupled from the yields of other government bonds and other comparable fixed-income markets. This created kinks in the government bond yield curve because targeted bonds remained relatively lower than yields of neighbouring bonds with similar maturities, which rose via the expectations channel.

In a similar vein to market liquidity, the impact of interventions on asset prices may depend on the scale of purchases by a central bank. Later rounds of asset purchases may

---

[3]The cash-futures basis is the spread between an asset's current price in the cash market and the price of the respective futures product.

have decreasing, or even inverse, impacts on prices compared with earlier rounds. Hesse, Hofmann, and Weber (2018) show that while facilities had initial positive impacts, subsequent extensions of these facilities had smaller results. In a starker result, Meaning and Zhu (2011) find that while sovereign bond yields declined by 30–80 basis points and 36–50 basis points around the initial announcements of the Fed's large-scale asset purchases and the BoE's asset purchase facilities, respectively, during the GFC, sovereign bond yields actually increased by several basis points upon the announcements of subsequent expansions of those facilities. With respect to equity prices, Harada and Okimoto (2021) show that the impact of the BoJ's exchange-traded fund (ETF) purchases on returns of eligible stocks relative to ineligible stocks waned over time. They find that on days the BoJ purchased ETFs, the returns of those stocks in the afternoon of the day, relative to stocks ineligible for the BoJ's facility, declined in the periods between each successive expansion of the facility, with an overall decline of 65% from 2013 to 2017.

Finally, another way in which a central bank may distort prices is by changing perceptions of market risk. Indeed, a central bank may wish to calm markets during a crisis by removing the possibility of tail-risk scenarios. Since assets are priced, in part, based on their potential risks, changes to these risks should result in similar changes to their prices. All else being equal, a reduction in a given asset's risk would generally be accompanied by an increase in that asset's value. Removal of the risk by the central bank can be controversial, since these actions can be seen as encouraging moral hazard on the part of market participants.

There is ample evidence in the literature that interventions distort prices through changes in various bond spreads. Gilchrist et al. (2020) and Boyarchenko, Kovner, and Shachar (2022) show that the Federal Reserve's Secondary Market Corporate Credit Facility (SMCCF) had different impacts on eligible bonds compared with their ineligible counterparts. Gilchrist et al. (2020) find that corporate bonds' credit risk premiums for eligible bonds declined by 47 basis points relative to ineligible bonds in a 2-day window around the announcement of the Fed's SMCCF and then declined to 28 basis points 10 days later. Boyarchenko, Kovner, and Shachar (2022) find that over a 3-day window around the Fed's announcement of the SMCCF, duration-matched credit spreads on A to AAA eligible bonds and BBB eligible bonds declined by 14.89 and 17.68 basis points per day relative to spreads of ineligible bonds. In Xu and Pennacchi (2023)'s analysis of the SMCCF they find a similar change in credit spreads, arguing that the exclusion criteria increased stigma around ineligible bonds. Boneva, De Roure, and Morley (2018) also find that the BoE's corporate purchase program reduced credit spreads of an issuer's eligible bonds by 13–14 basis points compared with the issuer's ineligible foreign bonds.

Finally, using options-implied tail risk, Haddad, Moreira, and Muir (2023) show that central bank programs reduce left-tail risk not only during but also after interventions, implying that participants internalize the possibility of future actions. Kelly, Lustig, and Van Nieuwerburgh (2016) find a similar reduction in tail risk associated with combinations of central bank programs and government stimulus measures during 2007 to 2009. They find that price deviations between out-of-the-money put options for financial sector ETFs and corresponding options on the underlying companies increase by 31% in the first five days following positive announcements of both central bank interventions and fiscal stimulus for the financial sector, demonstrating that the market perceived these interventions as sector-wide tail-risk insurance.

4 Conflicts between monetary policy and financial stability

Central bank interventions, whether in terms of asset purchases or lending, may be conducted under different objectives—principally, monetary policy or financial stability, with the latter sometimes being referred to as *market functioning*. For example, lender-of-last-resort-type operations may be used during the acute phase of a financial crisis to ensure solvent institutions are able to borrow against good collateral. Purchase operations may serve similar financial stability goals during the onset of a crisis but may also be used for monetary policy (as QE) during a prolonged period of low rates. When central banks take these actions, their objectives may come into conflict if they are responsible for both monetary policy and financial stability.

One way objectives could conflict is when financial stability and monetary policy actions act in opposite directions. For example, Lucca and Wright (2022) show that at the beginning of the COVID-19 crisis, the RBA's YCC program reinforced the central bank's forward guidance of maintaining low policy rates until inflation reverted to the target, which they did not expect for another three years. The two policies mutually reinforced one another such that the RBA was able to maintain its yield targets under the YCC with minimal actual purchases. However, once inflation rose and policy rate expectations were pulled forward, the RBA's YCC target was no longer consistent with the RBA's stated commitment to keep policy rates low. This resulted in the RBA purchasing large amounts of targeted government bonds shortly before discontinuing its YCC program. More recently, before the 2022 UK gilt crisis, the bank rate in the United Kingdom had begun increasing from a low of 0.10% before December 2021 to 1.75% in August 2022, representing a period of tightening. Following an initial unexpected increase in long-term gilt yields during September 2022, leveraged investors amplified such increases by selling long-term gilts for cash to meet larger margin requirements. The BoE was required to intervene to reduce yields on these same gilts and restore market functioning (Breeden 2022; Hauser 2020). The result was that BoE financial stability actions reduced long-term yields, albeit from a highly elevated position, during a period when they were increasing short-term yields. In that vein, Fleming et al. (2022) explain that market-function-type purchases can lead to unanticipated policy easing.

Alternatively, actions intended to impact one market may have unintended spillovers into others. Cimon and Walton (2022) show theoretically that central bank purchases of one asset type create similar impacts on other covariant assets through the dealer balance sheet channel.[4] Empirically, Morais et al. (2019) show that quantitative easing in the United States and United Kingdom created spillovers in Mexican markets, this time through the bank-lending channel.[5] In response to a one-standard-deviation increase in the Federal Reserve's assets relative to GDP, a proxy for QE, US banks operating in Mexico expanded credit volume by 2.5%, lengthened loan maturities by 7.1%, and experienced 6.5% higher future loan defaults. Moreover, one standard deviation in the proxy for QE leads to an 8.6% increase in future loan defaults for firms with loans that had higher than average ex-ante interest rates—evidence consistent with the interpretation that QE induced banks to engage in reach-for-yield behaviour by lending to riskier firms.

A third possibility is that asset purchases may interfere with the transmission of monetary policy. Pelizzon, Subrahmanyam, and Tomio (2023) show that ECB asset purchases induced scarcity in German and Italian government bonds, thereby increasing the costs of arbitrage, shown by a wider cash-futures basis, wider swap spreads and differences between model-fitted yields and observed yields across the term structure. This market inefficiency ultimately limited the pass-through of monetary policy from government bonds to other related assets by limiting the degree to which other assets responded to changes in government bond prices. Ballensiefen, Ranaldo, and Winterberg (2023) argue that, in another channel, ECB asset purchases created separation in repo markets between funding-driven and collateral-driven repos, where interest rates on the latter are less sensitive to the ECB's target benchmark repo rate. Bond scarcity induced by QE dampens this effect because the sensitivity of interest rates on repo transactions involving QE-eligible bonds to the ECB's benchmark repo rate was 17 basis points lower than for those involving non-eligible bonds. This led to higher dispersion among funding-driven and collateral-driven repo rates. Based on the notion that monetary policy should perfectly pass through to all money market rates (Corradin et al.

---

[4] The dealer balance sheet channel is the way by which dealers' balance sheet costs and frictions impact trading and prices in the markets they intermediate.

[5] The bank-lending channel is the method by which banks' lending choices impact financial markets and financial market participants.

2021), the higher dispersion among repo rates suggests the ECB had less control over the monetary policy transmission process.

5 Rent-seeking and other unproductive uses of central bank liquidity

A concern regarding interventions by central banks is that they can create opportunities for market intermediaries to extract economic rents, which are ultimately borne by investors and taxpayers. Dealers who intermediate over-the-counter (OTC) markets may find themselves with a new, reliable counterparty in the form of the central bank. This reliability is intentional, as it allows dealers to respond more efficiently to liquidity demand by their clients, preventing market dysfunction; however, it has costs. These costs typically arise from the design of auctions and facilities through which central banks implement their interventions.

One design choice that can create profit opportunities for dealers is the central bank's rules for allocating the auctioned amounts across dealers' bids. Song and Zhu (2018) suggest that since dealers could partially infer the specific bonds and prices that the Fed was willing to accept, dealers could short specific bonds into the Fed's QE auctions at a profit and later close their position in private markets. The authors estimate that one standard deviation in the "cheapness" of a bond (the bond's yield relative to a model-fitted yield) induced the Federal Reserve to purchase $276 million more of that bond and increased the auction cost on that bond by 2.6 cents per $100 par value. Similarly, Breedon (2018) finds that round-trip transaction costs, the difference between bond yields at auction and yields on days around the auction, equalled 0.5% of the total value of the BoE's QE program, and that some of this cost is attributed to dealers being able to exploit the allocation rules of the BoE's QE auctions.

Profit opportunities can also arise from the predictable trade sizes of the central bank and the publicly known set of dealers a central bank transacts with. An and Song (2023) estimate that, in the Fed's agency MBS auctions, dealers charged the Fed higher than private market clients by 2.5 cents per $100 par value, representing half of dealers' average gross profit margin. The authors find some evidence that this higher markup for the Fed was a result of the Fed's larger trade sizes compared with those of private market clients, and of the Fed's fixed set of dealer counterparties. In a study of the BoE's QE auctions, Boneva, Kastl, and Zikes (2020) suggest that dealers earned a rent of 2.6 basis points intermediating such auctions. The authors suggest that when a central bank intends to provide liquidity to dealers in an equitable way, no mechanism could fully eliminate these rents that dealers can extract due to their informational advantages.

Apart from intermediaries, security issuers may be enticed by the low rates caused by central banks' actions to engage in unproductive uses of liquidity provided by the central bank. Todorov (2020) shows that firms that issued bonds eligible for the ECB's CSPP used these issuances to increase corporate dividends four times higher in the two quarters following the announcement of the CSPP relative to the first quarter before the announcement. At the same time, the cash holdings, working capital, research and development, and property, plant and equipment accounts of these firms did not change. However, given data limitations, the authors caution against interpreting these results as purely a result of the ECB's CSPP. De Santis and Zaghini (2021) analyze the same program and show that while firms did increase investment in capital expenditures and intangibles, eligible firms also repurchased their own securities and held more cash. Darmouni and Siani (2022) show that corporations that were more exposed to the Fed's corporate credit facilities during the COVID-19 crisis were more likely to increase cash and less likely to increase real investments, perhaps because these firms were not initially financially constrained. Strikingly, for every dollar of new bonds issued, 45 cents were used to increase cash, 15 cents to pay back bank debt and 30 cents to refinance existing bonds, with no increase in real investment.

Firms may also use central bank facilities to increase leverage or to issue securities with riskier profiles. Indeed, Foley-Fisher, Ramcharan, and Yu (2016) show that, in response to the Fed's maturity extension program (MEP), firms with a preference for long-term debt, as proxied by the share of total debt that matures beyond three years, chose to issue additional long-term debt. During the MEP period, a one-standard-deviation increase in the authors' proxy for long-term debt preference corresponded to an 8 percentage point increase in long-term debt growth. Pegoraro and Montagna (2021) show that firms took advantage of decreased risk premiums and increased issuance of riskier bonds in response to the ECB's CSPP: more of these bonds were unsecured or non-guaranteed, with longer maturities, more fixed coupons and a more general (rather than specific) purpose. Bond characteristics aside, Acharya et al. (2022) show that in response to Fed QE programs during the GFC, firms vulnerable to a credit rating downgrade increased their bond issuance and used the proceeds to engage in more merger and acquisition activity. The authors show that this was riskier and prolonged rating downgrades that crystallized during the COVID-19 crisis.

Finally, interventions may simply be ineffective at improving market outcomes once banks become satisfied. These further interventions may incur costs but generate fewer benefits in exchange. Karadi and Nakov (2021) show that, once bank constraints are no longer binding, QE crowds out private lending and becomes ineffective at further easing credit conditions. Ertan, Kleymenova, and Tuijn (2020) show that banks that were more affected by the accumulated purchases through the ECB's CSPP increased their loans to small and medium-sized enterprises by 2% relative to the unaffected banks. However, these effects dissipated one year following the introduction of the ECB's CSPP.

6 Mitigation of costs and side effects

The existence of costs from central bank actions does not imply that central banks are unable to mitigate or manage them. On the contrary, central banks can take several actions to reduce these side effects. In a report prepared for the Bank for International Settlements Markets Committee, Logan and Bindseil (2019) categorize these mitigants into three groups:

- program design (purchase protocols, lending program protocols, transparency, minimizing uncertainty, minimizing information asymmetry and flexibility of implementation)
- securities-lending programs (primary, secondary and backstop)
- liability management practices and remuneration policies (absorbing excess liquidity, floor systems and reserve remuneration tiering)

In this section, we focus on program design and securities-lending programs.

A key element of program design is the choice and quantity of securities purchased by the central bank. When securities are purchased according to a specific index composition (e.g., price-weighted versus value-weighted), private markets may be distorted (Barbon and Gianinazzi 2019). Duffie and Keane (2023) argue that central banks can reduce distortion through the use of "delivery choice" reverse auction designs, which share some characteristics with "product mix auctions" (Klemperer 2010). In this design, central banks do not make offers on specific securities; instead, bidders are able to offer any eligible security at a spread to some maturity benchmark. Such a system can reduce inefficiencies from misallocated securities where scarcities exist among participants. They also argue in favour of transparent programs, which limit political economy costs and rent-seeking by eligible participants.

As a more specific measure, central banks may be able to mitigate collateral shortages and mispricing of specific bonds by engaging in securities-lending programs. Broadly speaking, these programs lend out securities on the central bank's balance sheet to market participants, increasing the supply of these securities in the private market. Use of these programs by the ECB has been shown to reduce bond scarcity that results from QE programs and increase the supply of collateral available in private markets (Pelizzon et al. 2023; Greppmair and Jank 2022). Similar programs in Canada have been shown to mitigate the negative consequences of settlement failures (Fontaine, Garriott, and Gray 2016).

In some circumstances, measures taken by central banks or financial market infrastructures treat the symptoms of these costs, rather than addressing the underlying costs themselves. One example of such a measure is a fail fee for repo transactions, where parties are charged a daily fee if they fail to deliver the security. Indeed, the introduction or increase of a fail fee has been shown to reduce the probability of failures to deliver (Corradin and Maddaloni 2020). However, such a fee simply discourages parties from failing to deliver bonds as a result of scarcity but does not resolve the bond scarcity itself.

7 Conclusion

It is clear from existing literature that, despite the benefits, there are unintended costs, distortions and side effects of central bank interventions. While it is possible that the benefits outweigh the costs, based on the extreme economic costs of financial crises, it is important for policy-makers to be cognizant of the large unintended consequences they may provoke. This paper set out to categorize these potential unintended costs and to review recent literature that provides evidence of their existence. The full economic impacts of these interventions are still not understood, and there is ample space for future work to that end.

Future work could analyze whether the side effects and unintended costs of central bank actions are attenuated or in fact exacerbated when they interact with NBFIs rather than dealers. Traditionally, central banks have often intervened through a network of bank-owned dealers. These dealers have played a central role in fixed-income markets and are often involved with central banks through mechanisms such as the issuance of government debt. Since these dealers are often subsidiaries of commercial banks, they are also highly regulated entities and may be viewed as relatively safe counterparties. However, the ultimate target of central bank actions may not be these dealers; instead, central banks may satisfy liquidity demand by NBFIs such as pension funds, insurance companies, mutual funds or hedge funds. Indeed, d'Avernas, Vandeweyer, and Darracq Paries (2020) argue that the existence of a large NBFI sector may limit the reach of traditional central bank programs. Some central banks have facilities that cater directly to these participants. For example, in 2020 the Bank of Canada introduced the Contingent Term Repo Facility to lend to non-bank counterparties, while in 2023 the Bank of England announced plans for lending tools for insurance companies and pension funds (Hauser 2023).

Another area of interest is the impact of changes to market structure on the costs of central bank actions. Traditionally, fixed-income securities were often traded exclusively through dealers with little transparency, even post-trade. If the securities targeted by central banks move toward an all-to-all market structure, are centrally cleared or are exchange traded, the balance of costs from these interventions could change. Alternatively, the size and scope of central bank interventions may be fundamentally different for primarily exchange-traded securities or securities that are intermediated by non-bank dealers.

References

Abidi, N. and I. Miquel-Flores. 2018. "Who Benefits from the Corporate QE? A Regression Discontinuity Design Approach." European Central Bank Working Paper No. 2145.

Acharya, V. V., R. Banerjee, M. Crosignani, T. Eisert and R. Spigt. 2022. "Exorbitant Privilege? Quantitative Easing and the Bond Market Subsidy of Prospective Fallen Angels." Federal Reserve Bank of New York Staff Report No. 29777.

An, Y. and Z. Song. 2023. "Does the Federal Reserve Obtain Competitive and Appropriate Prices in Monetary Policy Implementation?" *Review of Financial Studies* 36 (10): 4113–4157. https://doi.org/10.1093/rfs/hhad032.

Arrata, W., B. Nguyen, I. Rahmouni-Rousseau and M. Vari. 2020. "The Scarcity Effect of QE on Repo Rates: Evidence from the Euro Area." *Journal of Financial Economics* 137 (3): 837–856. https://doi.org/10.1016/j.jfineco.2020.04.009.

Bagehot, W. 1873. *Lombard Street: A Description of the Money Market*. London: H. S. King & Company.

Ballensiefen, B., A. Ranaldo and H. Winterberg. 2023. "Money Market Disconnect." *Review of Financial Studies* 36 (10): 4158–4189. https://doi.org/10.1093/rfs/hhad022.

Barbon, A. and V. Gianinazzi. 2019. "Quantitative Easing and Equity Prices: Evidence from the ETF Program of the Bank of Japan." *Review of Asset Pricing Studies* 9 (2): 210–255. https://doi.org/10.1093/rapstu/raz008.

Bernanke, B. S. 2022. *21st Century Monetary Policy: The Federal Reserve from the Great Inflation to COVID-19*. New York: W. W. Norton & Company.

Bessembinder, H., A. Carrion, L. Tuttle and K. Venkataraman. 2016. "Liquidity, Resiliency and Market Quality Around Predictable Trades: Theory and Evidence." *Journal of Financial Economics* 121 (1): 142–166. https://doi.org/10.1016/j.jfineco.2016.02.011.

Blinder, A., M. Ehrmann, J. de Haan and D.-J. Jansen. 2017. "Necessity as the Mother of Invention: Monetary Policy After the Crisis." *Economic Policy* 32 (92): 707–755. https://doi.org/10.1093/epolic/eix013.

Blix Grimaldi, M., A. Crosta and D. Zhang. 2021. "The Liquidity of the Government Bond Market—What Impact Does Quantitative Easing Have? Evidence from Sweden." Sveriges Riksbank Working Paper No. 402.

Boermans, M. and V. Keshkov. 2018. "The Impact of the ECB Asset Purchases on the European Bond Market Structure: Granular Evidence on Ownership Concentration." De Nederlandsche Bank Working Paper No. 590.

Boneva, L., C. de Roure and B. Morley. 2018. "The Impact of the Bank of England's Corporate Bond Purchase Scheme on Yield Spreads." Bank of England Working Paper No. 719.

Boneva, L., D. Elliott, I. Kaminska, O. Linton, N. McLaren and B. Morley. 2022. "The Impact of Corporate QE on Liquidity: Evidence from the UK." *Economic Journal* 132 (648): 2615–2643. https://doi.org/10.1093/ej/ueac033.

Boneva, L., M. Islami, and K. Schlepper. 2021. "Liquidity in the German Corporate Bond Market: Has the CSPP Made a Difference?" Deutsche Bundesbank Discussion Paper No. 08/2021. https://dx.doi.org/10.2139/ssrn.3813661.

Boneva, L., J. Kastl and F. Zikes. 2020. "Dealer Balance Sheets and bidding Behavior in the UK QE Reverse Auctions." Working Paper.

Boyarchenko, N., A. Kovner and O. Shachar. 2022. "It's What You Say and What You Buy: A Holistic Evaluation of the Corporate Credit Facilities." *Journal of Financial Economics* 144 (3): 695–731. https://doi.org/10.1016/j.jfineco.2022.03.001.

Breckenfelder, J. and M. Hoerova. 2023. "Do Non-Banks Need Access to the Lender of Last Resort? Evidence from Fund Runs." European Central Bank Working Paper No. 2805.

Breeden, S. 2022. "Risks from Leverage: How Did a Small Corner of the Pensions Industry Threaten Financial Stability?" Speech at ISDA and AIMA, London, November 7.

Breedon, F. 2018. "On the Transactions Costs of UK Quantitative Easing." *Journal of Banking & Finance* 88 (March): 347–356. https://doi.org/10.1016/j.jbankfin.2017.12.012.

Cimon, D. A. and A. Walton. 2022. "Central Bank Liquidity Facilities and Market Making." Bank of Canada Staff Working Paper No. 2022-9. https://doi.org/10.34989/swp-2022-9.

Corradin, S., J. Eisenschmidt, M. Hoerova, T. Linzert, G. Schepens and J.-D. Sigaux. 2021. "Money Markets, Central Bank Balance Sheet and Regulation." European Central Bank Working Paper No. 2483.

Corradin, S. and A. Maddaloni. 2020. "The Importance of Being Special: Repo Markets During the Crisis." *Journal of Financial Economics* 137 (2): 392–429. https://doi.org/10.1016/j.jfineco.2020.02.006.

D'Amico, S., R. Fan and Y. Kitsul. 2018. "The Scarcity Value of Treasury Collateral: Repo-Market Effects of Security-Specific Supply and Demand Factors." *Journal of Financial and Quantitative Analysis* 53 (5): 2103–2129.

Darmouni, O. and K. Siani. 2022. "Bond Market Stimulus: Firm-Level Evidence from 2020–21." CEPR Discussion Paper No. 17191.

d'Avernas, A., Q. Vandeweyer and M. Darracq Pariès. 2020. "Unconventional Monetary Policy and Funding Liquidity Risk." European Central Bank Working Paper No. 2350.

De Santis, R. A. and A. Zaghini. 2021. "Unconventional Monetary Policy and Corporate Bond Issuance." *European Economic Review* 135 (June): 103727. https://doi.org/10.1016/j.euroecorev.2021.103727.

Diamond, D. W. and R. G. Rajan. 2005. "Liquidity Shortages and Banking Crises." *Journal of Finance* 60 (2): 615–647.

Duffie, D. and F. M. Keane. 2023. "Market-Function Asset Purchases." Federal Reserve Bank of New York Staff Report No. 1054.

Ertan, A., A. Kleymenova and M. Tuijn. 2020. "Financial Intermediation Through Financial Disintermediation: Evidence from the ECB Corporate Sector Purchase Programme." Chicago Booth Research Paper No. 18-06. https://dx.doi.org/10.2139/ssrn.3197214.

Ferdinandusse, M., M. Freier and A. Ristiniemi. 2020. "Quantitative Easing and the Price-Liquidity Trade-Off." European Central Bank Working Paper No. 2399.

Fleming, M., H. Liu, R. Podjasek and J. Schurmeier. 2022. "The Federal Reserve's Market Functioning Purchases." Federal Reserve Bank of New York. *Economic Policy Review* 28 (1): 210–241.

Reprinted with the permission of the Bank of Canada, 2024.

Introduction

The 2024 edition of FP Bonds – Government, the ninth to be published by Grey House Publishing Canada, lists outstanding publicly and privately held debt securities, together with their features and provisions, issued by the Government of Canada, the provinces and selected federal and provincial agencies. All issues and amounts outstanding are as of Mar. 31, 2024, unless otherwise indicated. A Call Table appears at the end of each section listing the next call date and price for all callable bonds issued by the federal/provincial government or one of its agencies. An additional table lists all outstanding Eurobonds (Euro debt). Economic data on Canada and the provinces are provided as well as notes on Canadian taxation.

The formats for the three tables are as follows:

Main Body
- Cpn (%) – coupon rate (see Legend)
- Maturity date
- Frequency – frequency of interest payments (see Legend)
- Series
- CUSIP – CUSIP number
- Type – type of debt issued (see Legend)
- Year – year(s) of issue
- Amount (000) – total amount issued in original currency (see Legend)
- Outstanding Amount (000) - amount outstanding at Mar. 31, 2024, unless otherwise indicated
- Ref. Notes – numbered references which appear after the Call Table

Call Table
- Coupon Rate (%) – coupon rate (see Legend)
- Maturity date
- Next Call Date – date of next redemption
- Next Call Price – price at next redemption period
- Call Flag – flag indicating frequency of redemption
  - A (annual) – callable by the issuer on the day indicated and annually thereafter
  - C (continuous) – callable by issuer on or after Next Call Date
  - D (discrete) – callable by issuer on the day indicated
  - P (payment dates) – callable on day indicated plus subsequent interest payment dates

Eurobonds Table
- Cpn (%) – coupon rate (see Legend)
- Maturity date
- Frequency – frequency of interest payments (see Legend)
- Series
- Year – year(s) of issue
- Amount (000) – total amount issued in original currency (see Legend)
- Outstanding Amount (000) - amount outstanding at Mar. 31, 2024, unless otherwise indicated

Bond Ratings by Dominion Bond Rating Service are included on each issuer's title page.

Newly added front matter for this edition includes excerpts from the Bank of Canada's 2023 Annual Report, and a report on how central bank interventions during times of crisis can create strong benefits for financial systems.

Provincial Underwriters
Who takes which province to the market?

Province	Managers ■
Alberta	BMO-NB /CIBC/ /RBC-DS/S/TD (rotating lead managers)
British Columbia	BMO-NB /CIBC/ /RBC-DS/S/TD (rotating lead managers)
Manitoba	CIBC (lead manager)
	BMO-NB/RBC-DS (co-managers)
New Brunswick	BMO-NB/RBC-DS (rotating lead managers)
Newfoundland	RBC-DS/S (rotating lead managers)
	BMO-NB/CIBC/ML (co-managers)
Nova Scotia	BMO-NB/CIBC/RBC-DS/S (rotating lead managers)
Ontario	BMO-NB/CIBC/ML/ RBC-DS/S/TD (rotating lead managers)
P.E.I.	RBC-DS/S (rotating lead managers)
Québec	NBF (lead manager)
	BMO-NB/CIBC/ML/ RBC-DS/S (co-managers)
Saskatchewan	CIBC/RBC-DS (rotating lead managers)
	BMO-NB/S/TD (co-managers)

■ Managers are listed in alphabetical order; that may not be the same as participation in the account. Many of the managers are supported by other houses in underwriting the issues. The abbreviations above stand for:
BMO-NB– BMO Nesbitt Burns; CIBC – CIBC World Markets; ML – Merrill Lynch; NBF – National Bank Financial; RBC-DS – RBC Dominion Securities; S – Scotia Capital; TD – TD Securities.

British Columbia selects a lead for each deal, along with 2 co-leads, from BMO-NB, CIBC, RBC-DS, S and TD.

New Brunswick – One of CIBC, ML, NBF, S or TD is selected to join as a co-manager on each transaction.

Ontario selects a lead for each deal, along with 2 co-leads, from BMO-NB, CIBC, ML, RBC-DS, S and TD

Legend

Currency:
A$	Australian dollars
Ch¥	Chinese Yuan (offshore)
Cn¥	Chinese Yuan (onshore)
HK$	Hong Kong dollars
Jp¥	Japanese yen
Nkr	Norwegian Krone
NZ$	New Zealand dollars
R	South African Rand
SFr	Swiss francs
SKr	Swedish Krona
US$	United States dollars
€	Euros
£	British pound

Debt Type:
BD	Bonds
DB	Debentures
DN	Deposit Notes
EN	Equity-linked Notes
LN	Loans
MB	Mortgage Bonds
MN	Medium Term Notes
NT	Notes
SB	Serial Bonds
SV	Savings Bonds

Frequency:
A	Annually
M	Monthly
Q	Quarterly
S	Semiannually

Rate:
F.R.	Floating Rate
V.R.	Variable Rate
Var	Various
Z.R.	Zero Coupon Rate

Call Flag:
A	Annual
C	Continuous
D	Discrete
P	Payment Dates

Canadian Taxation

The following information, compiled from legislation, regulations, Department of Finance announcements and other published sources, is designed to give an outline of the various tax levies in Canada that, as of May 31, 2002 affect investments in debt obligations of or guaranteed by the Canadian Federal or Provincial Governments. Because the statutory provisions relating to the taxation of interest income and capital gains in Canada contain many special rules, all of which cannot be covered in this outline, the publisher and the author make no representation as to the accuracy or completeness of any of the following comments. Taxpayers are urged to consult their own tax advisors for advice relating to their own circumstances.

Government of Canada

Income Tax

(a) Residents of Canada

Under the federal Income Tax Act, in computing income for tax purposes, residents of Canada (individuals and corporations) must include all amounts received or receivable in respect of interest depending on the method regularly used by the taxpayer in calculating profit. Notwithstanding this general rule, taxpayers are required to include accrued interest annually on debt obligations to the extent not otherwise included in income.

Issuers of registered bonds or debentures are required to provide each year to the holders of their debt obligations a form (T-5 Supplementary) reporting the total payments of interest for that year or total interest accrued to the applicable anniversary date, as the case may be.

When a debt obligation is transferred, the transferor is required to include in income the interest accrued to the date of transfer and the transferee is allowed a corresponding deduction to the extent that such interest was otherwise included in the transferee's income.

One-half of capital gains from the sale of property, including securities, must be included in income of Canadian residents. One-half of realized capital losses may be deducted from the taxable portion of capital gains. There is provision for applying allowable capital losses against taxable capital gains of previous and subsequent taxation years. As a general rule, the gain realized by an investor on the maturity of a publicly traded interest bearing debt obligation purchased at a discount is a capital gain.

Investment dealers and financial institutions are required to recognize accrued gains and losses annually on their portfolio investments.

Discounts on interest bearing debt obligations issued by tax exempt entities, governments or other public bodies or non-residents not carrying on business in Canada will be income in the hands of the first Canadian resident non-exempt holder of such obligations if the effective yield exceeds the rate of interest by more than one-third in the case of obligations issued after June 18, 1971 and if the rate of interest is less than 5% in the case of obligations issued after December 20, 1960 and before June 19, 1971.

The Income Tax Regulations deem interest to accrue on non-interest bearing debt obligations (including stripped bonds) based on the yield. Those regulations also deem adjustments to the principal amount of indexed debt obligations (defined as obligations that are adjusted for changes in the purchasing power of money) to be interest.

Debt obligations that are convertible into shares or other debt obligations may qualify for rollover treatment so that no gain or loss would be realized on conversion.

There is a deemed disposition at fair market value of all capital property held by an individual on death. This may give rise to taxable capital gains and allowable capital losses. In the case of bequests to a spouse, or to a spouse trust, any such gains or losses may be postponed until the spouse disposes of the property. There is a similar deemed disposition in respect of specified capital property held by a resident of Canada upon becoming a non-resident.

Debt obligations of Canadian federal, provincial or municipal governments are eligible investments for registered retirement savings plans and other deferred income plans.

(b) Non-residents of Canada

The Income Tax Act provides for a withholding tax of 25% on interest (subject to certain exemptions) paid by a Canadian resident to any non-resident. This rate is reduced to 10% or 15% on payments to residents of most countries which have entered into tax treaties with Canada. The rate will depend upon the treaty. If the amount initially withheld and remitted on account of tax to the Receiver General at the time an interest payment is made to a non-resident exceeds the amount of tax payable (as limited by the appropriate tax treaty), the non-resident payee may apply to the Minister of National Revenue for a refund of the overpayment.

Debt obligations which are exempt from the withholding provisions on interest payments to non-residents include the following:

1. Bonds of or guaranteed by the Government of Canada issued on or before December 20, 1960.
2. Debt obligations of or guaranteed by Canadian federal, provincial and municipal governments issued after April 15, 1966.
3. Debt obligations of certain Canadian educational institutions, hospitals or government controlled corporations, commissions or associations issued after April 15, 1966.
4. Debt obligations issued before December 20, 1960, where the interest is neither payable in Canadian currency, nor by reference to Canadian currency.
5. Debt obligations issued after June 23, 1975 by corporations resident in Canada where the issue meets certain conditions respecting repayment.

Coupons on such tax exempt obligations issued after July 14, 1966 bear the designation "F". Coupons on obligations that are not exempt from withholding tax bear the designation "TX" if issued between March 29, 1961 and December 4, 1963, and the designation "AX" if issued after December 4, 1963. Anyone redeeming coupons on non-exempt obligations must withhold and remit to the Receiver General the appropriate amount on account of tax. There is also an exemption for interest paid by a prescribed financial institution that is the lender of an exempt government debt obligation under a securities lending arrangement.

The rate of withholding tax applicable to debt obligations of or guaranteed by a Province is 5% for issues on or before December 20, 1960 and for certain replacement issues subsequent to that date.

Trusts and organizations that are exempt from tax in their country of residence and that would be exempt if resident in Canada may obtain a certificate of exemption covering interest on debt obligations issued by arm's length obligors. Trusts or corporations which administer pension funds and charitable organizations may obtain such certificates of exemption even if they would not have exempt status in Canada provided they have exempt status in their country of residence.

Generally, unless debt obligations are used in the course of carrying on a business in Canada, a non-resident's capital gains from the disposition of a debt obligation will not be subject to Canadian income tax. However, if a non-resident sells a debt obligation to a Canadian resident at a premium above the issue price, the premium may be deemed to be a payment of interest and subject to withholding tax. Similarly, the sale of a debt obligation with accrued interest (whether actual or deemed) may result in a portion of the sale price being deemed to be a payment of interest to the extent of that accrued interest.

A non-resident of Canada may be able to claim the Canadian non-resident withholding tax as a credit against income taxes payable in his country of residence.

The Canada-United States Income Tax Convention contains a provision whereby the Canadian income of United States religious, scientific, literary, educational or charitable organizations is exempt from Canadian withholding tax to the extent that such income is exempt from income tax in the United States.

(c) Tax Treaties

The Government of Canada has negotiated or renegotiated tax treaties with the United States, United Kingdom, Algeria, Argentina, Australia, Austria, Bangladesh, Barbados, Belgium, Brazil, Bulgaria, Cameroon, Chile, China, Croatia, Cyprus, Czech Republic, Denmark, Dominican Republic, Egypt, Estonia, Finland, France, Germany, Guyana, Hungary, Iceland, India, Indonesia, Ireland, Israel, Italy, Ivory Coast, Jamaica, Japan, Jordan, Kazakhstan, Kenya, Kyrgyzstan, Latvia, Lebanon, Lithuania, Luxembourg, Malaysia, Malta, Mexico, Morocco, Netherlands, New Zealand, Nigeria, Norway, Pakistan, Papua New Guinea, Philippines, Poland, Portugal, Romania, Russian Federation, Singapore, Slovakia, South Africa, South Korea, Spain, Sri Lanka, Sweden, Switzerland, Tanzania, Thailand, Trinidad and Tobago, Tunisia, Ukraine, Uzbekistan, Vietnam, Zambia and Zimbabwe. In some cases, the tax treaty may not have been implemented by the enabling legislation or proclaimed in force either in Canada or the other treaty country, and consequently, specific inquiries should be made with respect to recently negotiated treaties.

Estate Tax

The estate tax imposed by the Government of Canada was repealed effective January 1, 1972, and, from that date, the only Federal tax liability arising on death pertains to the liability under the Income Tax Act arising from the deemed disposition of capital property referred to above.

Goods and Services Tax

The Federal Government enacted legislation implementing the goods and services tax effective January 1, 1991. Interest on debt obligations and proceeds from the sale of debt obligations are exempt from that tax.

Provincial Governments

Income and Corporation Taxes

All of the provinces of Canada have enacted income tax statutes. Generally, whether an individual or corporation is liable to taxation under any one or more of such statutes will depend on whether or not the individual or corporation was resident in or had a permanent establishment in a province during the year.

Capital Taxes

Canada and all the Provinces, except Alberta, Newfoundland and Prince Edward Island, impose a capital tax on corporations. Subject to meeting various term and hold conditions, investments in the debt obligations of other corporations (including Crown corporations) reduce a corporation's taxable capital. Except for Manitoba and Saskatchewan, investments in government debt obligations do not reduce taxable capital.

Succession Duties

All provinces have withdrawn from the field of succession duties.

Notes prepared by Eric G. Nazzer

Canada

Details of debt issued by the Government of
Canada and its federal agencies, listed by maturity date.
Information on Canadian Savings Bonds.

Canada

Prime Minister: Justin Trudeau, Liberal Party of Canada
Capital City: Ottawa
Area: 9,984,670 sq. kilometres

Visit these Web sites:
Government of Canada: www.canada.gc.ca
Export Development Canada: www.edc.ca

DBRS Bond Rating at March 7, 2024 ... AAA

	2023	2022
GDP, by inc. & expend. (at market)	$2,375,770,000,000	$2,216,812,000,000
Employed (Dec.)	20,324,900	19,882,300
Unemployed (Dec.)	1,243,800	1,043,400
Average weekly earnings (Dec.)	$1,211.79	$1,173.9
December consumer price index (2002=100)	158.3	153.1
Building permits	$132,200,383,000	$135,368,792,000
Merchandise exports	$768,272,100,000	$779,108,600,000
Merchandise imports	$770,401,700,000	$756,836,100,000
Retail sales	$794,404,142,000	$735,792,059,000
Farm cash receipts	$98,576,880	$94,885,100,000
Population (est. July 1)	40,097,761	38,929,902
Index of gross domestic product at market prices (2017=100)	122.9	127.6
Raw materials price index (excl. crude energy products) (annual avg., 2020=100)	135.8	136.5
Crude energy products price index (annual avg., 2020=100)	145.8	177.3
Industrial product price index, manufacturing (annual avg., 2020=100)	125.7	128

DIRECT DEBT
March 31, 2024

Cpn %	Maturity	Freq	Series	CUSIP	Type	Year	Issued Amount (000)	Outstanding Amount (000)	Ref. Note
GOVERNMENT OF CANADA									
0.250	2024.04.01	S	L690	135087L69	BD	'20-'21	$37,000,000	$36,980,000	
1.500	2024.05.01	S		135087N42	BD	2022	$16,000,000	$15,800,000	
2.500	2024.06.01	S	B451	135087B45	BD	'13-'14	$13,800,000	$13,700,000	
2.750	2024.08.01	S		135087N91	BD	2022	$16,500,000	$14,075,000	
1.500	2024.09.01	S	J967	135087J96	BD	2019	$16,200,000	$16,065,381	1
0.750	2024.10.01	S		135087M50	BD	2021	$14,000,000	$14,000,000	
3.000	2024.11.01	S		135087P40	BD	2022	$16,000,000	$14,400,000	
1.625	2025.01.22	S		135087K78	BD	2020	US$3,000,000	US$3,000,000	
3.750	2025.02.01	S		135087P65	BD	'22-'23	$15,000,000	$14,750,000	
1.250	2025.03.01	S	K528	135087K52	BD	'19-'20	$16,800,000	$17,300,000	
1.500	2025.04.01	S		135087N34	BD	2022	$12,000,000	$11,875,000	
2.875	2025.04.28	S		135087N75	BD	2022	US$3,500,000	US$3,500,000	
3.750	2025.05.01	S		135087Q31	BD	2023	$15,250,000	$15,250,000	
9.000	2025.06.01	S	A76	135087VH4	BD	'94-'96	$8,900,000	$2,133,858	
2.250	2025.06.01	S	D507	135087D50	BD	'14-'15	$13,100,000	$13,100,000	
3.500	2025.08.01	S		135087Q64	BD	2023	$19,000,000	$19,000,000	
0.500	2025.09.01	S	K940	135087K94	BD	2020	$47,500,000	$47,500,000	
3.000	2025.10.01	S		135087P24	BD	2022	$10,000,000	$10,000,000	
4.500	2025.11.01	S		135087Q80	BD	2023	$19,750,000	$19,750,000	
4.500	2026.02.01	S		135087R22	BD	'23-'24	$23,000,000	$23,000,000	
0.250	2026.03.01	S	L518	135087L51	BD	'20-'21	$34,000,000	$34,000,000	
3.000	2026.04.01	S		135087P81	BD	2023	$10,000,000	$10,000,000	
4.000	2026.05.01	S		135087R55	BD	2024	$19,500,000	$26,000,000	
0.750	2026.05.19	S		427028AB1	BD	2021	US$3,500,000	US$3,500,000	
1.500	2026.06.01	S	E679	135087E67	BD	'15-'16	$13,500,000	$13,472,000	
1.000	2026.09.01	S	L930	135087L93	BD	2021	$23,000,000	$23,000,000	
4.250	2026.12.01	S	VS05	135087VS0	BD	'95-'98	$5,250,000	$5,250,000	2
1.250	2027.03.01	S		135087M84	BD	'21-'22	$17,000,000	$17,000,000	
1.000	2027.06.01	S	F825	135087F82	BD	'16-'17	$15,000,000	$14,740,000	
8.000	2027.06.01	S	VW17	135087VW1	BD	'96-'97	$9,600,000	$3,620,841	
3.245	2027.08.24	S		135087P73	BD	2022	$500,000	$500,000	1
2.750	2027.09.01	S		135087N83	BD	2022	$16,000,000	$16,000,000	
3.500	2028.03.01	S		135087P57	BD	'22-'23	$15,000,000	$15,000,000	
3.750	2028.04.26	S		135087Q56	BD	2023	US$4,000,000	US$4,000,000	
2.000	2028.06.01	S	H235	135087H23	BD	'17-'18	$13,500,000	$13,500,000	
3.250	2028.09.01	S		135087Q49	BD	2023	$20,000,000	$20,000,000	
4.000	2029.03.01	S		135087Q98	BD	'23-'24	$27,000,000	$27,000,000	
2.250	2029.06.01	S	J397	135087J39	BD	'18-'19	$12,300,000	$12,300,000	
5.750	2029.06.01	S	WL43	135087WL4	BD	'98-'01	$13,900,000	$10,598,959	
2.250	2029.12.01	S		135087N67	BD	2022	$5,000,000	$5,000,000	3
1.250	2030.06.01	S	K379	135087K37	BD	'19-'20	$44,200,000	$44,200,000	
0.500	2030.12.01	S	L443	135087L44	BD	'20-'21	$40,000,000	$40,000,000	
1.500	2031.06.01	S	M276	135087M27	BD	2021	$42,000,000	$42,000,000	
1.500	2031.12.01	S		135087N26	BD	'21-'22	$32,000,000	$32,000,000	
4.000	2031.12.01	S	WW25	135087WV2	BD	'99-'03	$5,800,000	$5,800,000	2
2.000	2032.06.01	S		135087N59	BD	2022	$24,000,000	$24,000,000	

FP Bonds — Government 2024

Canada

Cpn %	Maturity	Freq	Series	CUSIP	Type	Year	Issued Amount (000)	Outstanding Amount (000)	Ref. Note
2.500	2032.12.01	S		135087P32	BD	2022	$21,000,000	$21,000,000	
2.750	2033.06.01	S		135087Q23	BD	2023	$19,000,000	$19,000,000	
5.750	2033.06.01	S	XG49	135087XG4	BD	'01-'04	$13,410,295	$11,988,905	
3.250	2033.12.01	S		135087Q72	BD	2023	$21,000,000	$21,000,000	
3.500	2034.03.01	S		135087R71	BD	2024	$4,000,000	$4,000,000	3
3.000	2034.06.01	S		135087R48	BD	'23-'24	$14,000,000	$29,000,000	
3.000	2036.12.01	S	XQ21	135087XQ2	BD	'03-'07	$5,850,000	$5,850,000	2
5.000	2037.06.01	S	XW98	135087XW9	BD	'04-'09	$13,999,089	$11,730,774	
4.000	2041.06.01	S	YQ12	135087YQ1	BD	'08-'11	$15,800,000	$13,838,441	
2.000	2041.12.01	S	YK42	13522ZYK4	BD	'07-'10	$6,550,000	$6,550,000	2
1.500	2044.12.01	S	ZH04	135087ZH0	BD	'10-'13	$7,700,000	$7,700,000	2
3.500	2045.12.01	S	ZS68	135087ZS6	BD	'11-'14	$16,400,000	$16,300,000	
1.250	2047.12.01	S	B949	135087B94	BD	'13-'17	$7,700,000	$7,700,000	2
2.750	2048.12.01	S	D358	135087D35	BD	'14-'17	$14,900,000	$14,900,000	
0.500	2050.12.01	S	G997	135087G99	BD	'17-'21	$7,600,000	$7,600,000	2
2.000	2051.12.01	S	H722	135087H72	BD	'17-'21	$49,700,000	$51,816,529	
1.750	2053.12.01	S		135087M68	BD	'21-'22	$32,000,000	$32,000,000	
0.250	2054.12.01	S		135087M43	BD	'21-'22	$2,100,000	$2,100,000	
2.750	2055.12.01	S		135087P99	BD	'23-'24	$16,750,000	$18,750,000	
2.750	2064.12.01	S	C939	135087C93	BD	'14-'22	$8,750,000	$8,750,000	

GUARANTEED DEBT
March 31, 2024

Cpn %	Maturity	Freq	Series	CUSIP	Type	Year	Issued Amount (000)	Outstanding Amount (000)	Ref. Note
CPPIB CAPITAL INC.									
3.000	2024.06.13	S	50	22411VAW8	SN	2022	US$600,000	US$600,000	
0.750	2024.06.15	S		12593CAP6	NT	2020	$500,000	$500,000	
0.375	2024.06.20	A			BD	2017	€2,000,000	€2,000,000	
F.R.	2024.07.29	Q	41	22411VAT5	BD	2021	US$250,000	US$250,000	
0.500	2024.09.16	S	34	22411VAR9	NT	2021	US$1,000,000	US$1,000,000	
4.125	2024.10.21	S	52	22411VAY4	NT	2022	US$1,750,000	US$1,750,000	
0.875	2024.12.17	A	17		NT	2020	£500,000	£500,000	
1.250	2025.03.04	S	18	22411VAM0	NT	2020	US$1,000,000	US$1,000,000	
F.R.	2025.04.04	Q	47	22411WAU0	NT	2022	US$1,500,000	US$1,500,000	
6.000	2025.06.07	A	58		NT	2023	£1,000,000	£1,000,000	
0.375	2025.07.29	S	26	22411VAP3	NT	2020	US$1,000,000	US$1,000,000	
3.950	2025.09.08	S	53	C28009AF2	NT	2022	$500,000	$500,000	
4.400	2026.01.16	S			NT	'23-'24	A$1,500,000	A$1,500,000	
4.375	2026.03.02	A	56		SN	2023	£750,000	£750,000	
F.R.	2026.03.11	Q	40	12593CAQ4	SN	2021	US$750,000	US$750,000	
F.R.	2026.06.15	Q	37		NT	2021	£750,000	£750,000	
4.100	2026.09.01	S	4		MN	2023	A$500,000	A$500,000	
0.875	2026.09.09	S	42	22411VAU2	MN	2021	US$2,500,000	US$2,500,000	
4.375	2027.01.31	S	62	22411VBA5	NT	2024	US$1,250,000	US$1,250,000	
0.250	2027.04.06	A	19		MN	2020	€1,000,000	€1,000,000	
F.R.	2027.04.27	Q	49		SN	2022	£300,000	£300,000	
2.850	2027.06.01	S	48	12593CAT8	NT	2022	$1,500,000	$1,500,000	

Cpn %	Maturity	Freq	Series	CUSIP	Type	Issued Year	Issued Amount (000)	Outstanding Amount (000)	Ref. Note
3.250	2027.06.15	S	51	22411WAW6	NT	2022	US$1,500,000	US$1,500,000	
4.500	2027.07.22	A	63		NT	2024	£600,000	£600,000	
4.450	2027.09.01	S			NT	'22-'23	A$1,350,000	A$1,350,000	
2.750	2027.11.02	S	4	22411VAD0	NT	2017	US$1,000,000	US$1,000,000	
1.250	2027.12.07	A	44		MN	2022	£600,000	£600,000	
3.250	2028.03.08	S	57	12593CAV3	NT	2023	$3,000,000	$3,000,000	
4.200	2028.05.02	S			NT	2023	A$1,600,000	A$1,600,000	
3.000	2028.06.15	S	8	12593CAF8	NT	'18-'22	$2,500,000	$2,500,000	
1.500	2028.06.23	S	38		NT	2021	A$750,000	A$750,000	
4.250	2028.07.20	S	59	22411VAZ1	NT	2023	US$1,500,000	US$1,500,000	
4.400	2029.01.15	S			NT	2024	A$1,500,000	A$1,500,000	
0.875	2029.02.06	A	12		NT	2019	€1,000,000	€1,000,000	
3.600	2029.06.02	S	61	12593CAX9	NT	2024	$1,700,000	$2,200,000	
1.950	2029.09.30	S	14	12593CAJ0	BD	2019	$1,000,000	$1,000,000	
2.000	2029.11.01	S	15	22411WAK2	NT	2019	US$1,000,000	US$1,000,000	
1.125	2029.12.14	A	23		SN	2020	£750,000	£750,000	
1.250	2031.01.28	S	29	22411WAQ9	NT	2021	US$1,000,000	US$1,000,000	
0.050	2031.02.24	A	31		MN	2021	€1,000,000	€1,000,000	
2.250	2031.12.01	S	45	12593CAR2	NT	2022	$1,400,000	$1,400,000	
3.950	2032.06.02	S	55	12593ZAA8	NT	2023	$3,700,000	$3,700,000	
1.500	2033.03.04	A	6		NT	2018	€1,000,000	€1,000,000	
4.750	2033.06.02	S	60	12593CAW1	NT	'23-'24	$2,200,000	$3,000,000	
5.200	2034.03.04	S			NT	2024	A$1,500,000	A$1,500,000	
0.750	2037.02.02	A	46		MN	2022	€1,000,000	€1,000,000	
0.250	2041.01.18	A	28		NT	2021	€1,000,000	€1,000,000	
2.414	2041.02.25	S			MN	2021	A$150,000	A$150,000	
2.790	2041.03.12	S	33		MN	2021	A$120,000	A$120,000	
2.565	2041.04.23	A			MN	2021	A$110,000	A$110,000	
0.750	2049.07.15	A	13		NT	2019	€1,000,000	€1,000,000	
2.580	2051.02.23	S	30		MN	2021	A$160,000	A$160,000	
1.625	2071.10.22	A	43		NT	2021	£900,000	£900,000	
CPPIB REAL ESTATE HOLDINGS INC.									
3.752	2025.06.10	M	A	12593EAA5	MB	2015	$175,000	$137,030	
CANADA HOUSING TRUST									
2.900	2024.06.15	S	58	13509PEF6	MB	'14-'19	$17,000,000	$17,000,000	
F.R.	2024.09.15	Q	89	13509PHE6	MB	2019	$5,000,000	$5,000,000	
1.800	2024.12.15	S	90	13509PHJ5	MB	2019	$10,500,000	$10,500,000	
2.550	2025.03.15	S	62	13509PER0	MB	'14-'15	$5,500,000	$5,500,000	
F.R.	2025.03.15	Q	91	13509PHL0	MB	'19-'20	$4,250,000	$4,250,000	
0.950	2025.06.15	S	93	13509PHN6	MB	2020	$12,000,000	$12,000,000	
F.R.	2025.09.15	Q	94	13509PHP1	MB	2020	$2,000,000	$2,000,000	
1.950	2025.12.15	S	67	13509PFA6	MB	'15-'20	$13,000,000	$13,000,000	
2.250	2025.12.15	S	70	13509PFD0	MB	'15-'16	$4,000,000	$4,000,000	
F.R.	2026.03.15	Q	96	13509PHR7	MB	'20-'21	$3,000,000	$3,000,000	
1.250	2026.06.15	S	98	13509PHT3	MB	2021	$10,000,000	$10,000,000	
1.900	2026.09.15	S	73	13509PFL2	MB	2016	$7,000,000	$7,000,000	
F.R.	2026.09.15	Q	99	13509PHV8	MB	2021	$2,250,000	$2,250,000	
1.100	2026.12.15	S	102	13509PHX4	MB	2021	$5,250,000	$5,250,000	
1.550	2026.12.15	S	105	13509PJA2	MB	2021	$5,000,000	$5,000,000	
F.R.	2027.03.15	Q	103	13509PHY2	MB	'21-'22	$2,000,000	$2,000,000	

Cpn %	Maturity	Freq	Series	CUSIP	Type	Year	Issued Amount (000)	Outstanding Amount (000)	Ref. Note
3.800	2027.06.15	S	109	13509PJE4	MB	2022	$5,000,000	$5,000,000	
2.350	2027.06.15	S	77	13509PFX6	MB	'17-'22	$12,250,000	$12,250,000	
F.R.	2027.09.15	Q	108	13509PJD6	MB	2022	$2,500,000	$2,500,000	
3.600	2027.12.15	S	110	13509PJF1	MB	2022	$10,000,000	$10,000,000	
F.R.	2028.03.15	Q	111	13509PJG9	MB	'22-'23	$2,500,000	$2,500,000	
2.350	2028.03.15	S	80	13509PGF4	MB	2017	$2,500,000	$2,500,000	
2.650	2028.03.15	S	82	13509PGL1	MB	2018	$4,250,000	$4,250,000	
3.100	2028.06.15	S	113	13509PJL8	MB	2023	$5,000,000	$5,000,000	
3.950	2028.06.15	S	115	13509PJN4	MB	2023	$5,000,000	$5,000,000	
F.R.	2028.09.15	Q	114	13509PJM6	MB	2023	$2,250,000	$2,250,000	
4.250	2028.12.15	S	117	13509PJQ7	MB	2023	$11,000,000	$11,000,000	
2.650	2028.12.15	S	85	13509PGS6	MB	'18-'19	$6,500,000	$6,500,000	
F.R.	2029.03.15	Q	119	13509PJR5	MB	'23-'24	$1,000,000	$1,000,000	
3.700	2029.06.15	S	120	13509PJT1	MB	2024	$8,000,000	$8,000,000	
2.100	2029.09.15	S	88	13509PHD8	MB	2019	$6,750,000	$6,750,000	
1.750	2030.06.15	S	92	13509PHM8	MB	2020	$10,750,000	$10,750,000	
1.900	2031.03.15	S	100	13509PHU0	MB	2021	$3,500,000	$3,500,000	
1.100	2031.03.15	S	95	13509PHQ9	MB	2020	$4,250,000	$4,250,000	
1.400	2031.03.15	S	97	13509PHS5	MB	2021	$4,000,000	$4,000,000	
1.600	2031.12.15	S	101	13509PHW6	MB	2021	$4,000,000	$4,000,000	
2.150	2031.12.15	S	104	13509PHZ9	MB	2021	$4,000,000	$4,000,000	
2.450	2031.12.15	S	106	13509PJB0	MB	2022	$3,750,000	$3,750,000	
3.550	2032.09.15	S	107	13509PJC8	MB	2022	$11,000,000	$11,000,000	
3.650	2033.06.15	S	112	13509PJK0	MB	2023	$8,000,000	$8,000,000	
4.150	2033.06.15	S	116	13509PJP9	MB	2023	$4,000,000	$4,000,000	
4.250	2034.03.15	S	118	13509PJS3	MB	'23-'24	$15,000,000	$22,000,000	
EXPORT DEVELOPMENT CANADA									
F.R.	2024.04.04	Q		30216BJC7	NT	2021	US$250,000	US$250,000	
0.500	2024.04.08	Q		30216BJB9	NT	2021	US$250,000	US$250,000	
1.650	2024.07.31	S		30216BHL9	BD	2019	$500,000	$500,000	3
0.610	2024.10.28	S		30216BJF0	MN	2021	US$250,000	US$250,000	
0.677	2025.02.28	S			MN	2021	US$250,000	US$250,000	
3.375	2025.08.26	S		30216BJU7	BD	2022	US$3,250,000	US$3,250,000	
2.720	2025.09.13	A			MN	2022	Ch¥1,000,000	Ch¥1,000,000	
2.600	2026.01.17	A			MN	2023	Ch¥1,000,000	Ch¥1,000,000	
1.050	2026.05.26	S		30216BJP8	NT	2021	US$200,000	US$200,000	
4.375	2026.06.29	S		30216BKB7	BD	2023	US$2,000,000	US$2,000,000	
4.400	2027.01.22	S			NT	2023	A$1,000,000	A$1,000,000	
3.000	2027.05.25	S		30216BJR4	BD	2022	US$2,750,000	US$2,750,000	
3.875	2028.02.14	S		30216BJW3	BD	2023	US$3,500,000	US$3,500,000	
4.500	2028.09.06	S			BD	2023	A$1,000,000	A$1,000,000	
4.125	2029.02.13	S		30216BKC5	NT	2024	US$3,500,000	US$3,500,000	
4.500	2029.08.08	S			NT	2024	A$1,000,000	A$1,000,000	

CALLABLE BONDS
March 31, 2024

Coupon Rate %	Maturity Date	Next Call Date	Next Call Price	Call Flag
CPPIB REAL ESTATE HOLDINGS INC.				
3.752	2025.06.10	anytime	$100.00	C

REFERENCES
1. Ukraine Sovereignty Bonds.
2. Real return bonds. The bonds bear interest adjusted in relation to the Consumer Price Index for Canada. Interest consists of both an inflation compensation component calculated based on principal and payable at maturity and a cash entitlement calculated based on principal and accrued inflation compensation. Coupon interest is payable semiannually. At maturity, in addition to coupon interest payable on such date, a final payment equal to the sum of principal plus inflation compensation accrued from the original issue date to maturity will be made.
3. Green bonds.

Treasury Bills

Maturity Date 2024	Issue Date 2023	Average Price	Average Yield	Outstanding $000,000
Jan. 4	Jan. 5	95.549	4.671	3,400
Jan. 4	Jan. 19	95.797	4.575	3,400
Jan. 4	Sept. 28	98.637	5.145	13,400
Jan. 18	July 20	97.490	5.164	4,400
Jan. 18	Aug. 3	97.662	5.201	4,800
Jan. 18	Oct. 12	98.635	5.155	11,600
Feb. 1	Feb. 2	95.653	4.557	3,800
Feb. 1	Feb. 16	95.613	4.785	3,800
Feb. 1	Oct. 26	98.633	5.161	11,600
Feb. 15	Aug. 17	97.463	5.221	5,200
Feb. 15	Aug. 31	97.654	5.219	5,400
Feb. 15	Nov. 9	98.663	5.046	11,600
Feb. 29	Mar. 2	95.472	4.756	3,800
Feb. 29	Mar. 16	96.002	4.343	3,800
Feb. 29	Nov. 23	98.664	5.042	11,600
Mar. 14	Sept. 14	97.485	5.173	5,200
Mar. 14	Sept. 28	97.642	5.246	4,800
Mar. 14	Dec. 7	98.670	5.020	11,600
Mar. 28	Mar. 30	95.846	4.346	3,800
Mar. 28	Apr. 13	95.892	4.468	4,200
Mar. 28	Dec. 21	98.666	5.037	11,600
Apr. 11	Oct. 12	97.455	5.238	4,200
Apr. 11	Oct. 26	97.657	5.212	4,200
Apr. 11	Jan. 4	98.665	5.041	11,600
Apr. 25	Apr. 27	95.751	4.450	4,600
Apr. 25	May 11	95.856	4.508	4,200
Apr. 25	Jan. 18	98.665	5.041	12,200
May 9	Nov. 9	97.536	5.067	4,200
May 9	Nov. 23	97.730	5.047	4,200
May 9	Feb. 1	98.667	5.031	12,200
May 23	May 25	95.474	4.754	4,800
May 23	June 8	95.444	4.978	4,200
May 23	Feb. 15	98.667	5.032	14,000
June 6	Dec. 7	97.589	4.955	4,200
June 6	Dec. 21	97.754	4.991	4,200
June 6	Feb. 29	98.680	4.981	14,000
June 20	June 22	95.070	5.200	4,200
June 20	July 6	95.271	5.177	4,200
June 20	Mar. 14	98.691	4.940	14,000
July 4	Jan. 4	97.582	4.970	4,200
July 4	Jan. 18	97.758	4.982	4,400
July 4	Mar. 28	98.676	4.999	15,800
July 18	July 20	95.054	5.218	4,400
July 18	Aug. 3	95.179	5.282	4,800
July 18	Apr. 11	98.681	4.980	14,000
Aug. 1	Feb. 1	97.575	4.984	4,400
Aug. 1	Feb. 15	97.731	5.044	5,000
Aug. 15	Aug. 17	94.980	5.300	5,200
Aug. 15	Aug. 31	95.190	5.270	5,400

Treasury Bills

Maturity Date 2024	Issue Date 2023	Average Price	Average Yield	Outstanding $000,000
Aug. 29	Feb. 29	97.576	4.983	5,000
Aug. 29	Mar. 14	97.773	4.948	5,000
Sept. 12	Sept. 14	95.047	5.225	5,200
Sept. 12	Sept. 28	95.118	5.352	4,800
Sept. 26	Mar. 28	97.596	4.940	5,600
Sept. 26	Apr. 11	97.793	4.904	5,000
Oct. 10	Oct. 12	94.981	5.299	4,200
Oct. 10	Oct. 26	95.217	5.238	4,200
Nov. 7	Nov. 9	95.250	5.001	4,200
Nov. 7	Nov. 23	95.473	4.945	4,200
Dec. 5	Dec. 7	95.498	4.727	4,200
Dec. 5	Dec. 21	95.681	4.707	4,200
Total				**395,600**

Provincial Debt

Details of debt issued by Canadian provinces and their agencies.

Alberta

Premier: Danielle Smith (United Conservative Party)
Capital City: Edmonton
Area: 661,848 sq. kilometres

Visit these Web sites:
  Province of Alberta: www.alberta.ca
  Alberta Capital Finance Authority: www.acfa.gov.ab.ca

DBRS Bond Rating at September 14, 2023 ... AA

	2023	2022
Employed	2,502,600	2,409,000
Unemployment rate (%)	6.3	5.6
Average weekly earnings (Dec.)	$1,291.41	$1,268.07
Building permits	$15,772,620,000	$15,367,989,000
Retail sales	$102,122,841,000	$95,074,490,000
Population (est. July 1)	4,695,290	4,543,111
December consumer price index (2002=100)	165.6	160.8
Sales tax (GST)	5%	5%

DIRECT DEBT
March 31, 2024

Cpn %	Maturity	Freq	Series	CUSIP	Type	Year	Issued Amount (000)	Outstanding Amount (000)	Ref. Note
PROVINCE OF ALBERTA									
3.100	2024.06.01	S		013051DM6	NT	'14-'21	$2,833,000	$2,833,000	
1.875	2024.11.13	S		013051EH6	BD	2019	US$2,250,000	US$2,250,000	
0.500	2025.04.16	A			NT	2020	€1,100,000	€1,100,000	
0.625	2025.04.18	A			NT	2018	€1,500,000	€1,500,000	
1.000	2025.05.20	S		013051EK9	BD	2020	US$2,250,000	US$2,250,000	
2.350	2025.06.01	S	DJ	013051DQ7	DB	'15-'20	$3,700,000	$3,700,000	
0.625	2026.01.16	A			NT	2019	€1,250,000	€1,250,000	
4.300	2026.06.01	S		01306ZCP4	NT	2011	$30,000	$30,000	
2.200	2026.06.01	S		013051DT1	NT	'16-'20	$3,700,000	$3,700,000	
2.050	2026.08.17	S	PAGM06	01306GAC7	NT	2016	US$1,000,000	US$1,000,000	
3.100	2026.12.14	S			NT	'16-'18	A$505,000	A$505,000	
2.550	2027.06.01	S		013051DW4	NT	'17-'20	$5,700,000	$5,700,000	
3.300	2028.03.15	S		013051EA1	BD	2018	US$1,250,000	US$1,250,000	
3.600	2028.04.11	S			NT	'17-'19	A$460,000	A$460,000	
0.250	2028.04.20	A			NT	2020	SFr260,000	SFr260,000	
2.900	2028.12.01	S		013051EB9	DB	'18-'19	$3,300,000	$3,300,000	
0.375	2029.02.07	A			MN	2019	SFr325,000	SFr325,000	
1.403	2029.02.20	A			NT	2019	SKr2,500,000	SKr2,500,000	
2.900	2029.09.20	S		01306ZCV1	NT	'12-'20	$2,062,700	$2,062,700	
2.050	2030.06.01	S		013051EG8	DB	'19-'20	$8,100,000	$8,100,000	
1.300	2030.07.22	S		013051EM5	DB	2020	US$2,000,000	US$2,000,000	
2.400	2030.10.02	S			MN	2020	A$170,000	A$170,000	
3.500	2031.06.01	S		01306ZDF5	NT	2014	$1,230,000	$1,230,000	
1.650	2031.06.01	S		013051EP8	BD	2021	$3,500,000	$3,500,000	
4.150	2033.06.01	S		013051ER4	BD	'22-'24	$2,750,000	$2,750,000	
3.900	2033.12.01	S		01306ZDC2	NT	'13-'21	$1,815,000	$1,815,000	
4.500	2034.01.24	S		013051ET0	BD	2024	US$1,250,000	US$1,250,000	
2.010	2036.02.19	S			MN	2021	A$200,000	A$200,000	
4.500	2040.12.01	S		013051DB0	BD	2010	$600,000	$600,000	
1.782	2040.12.03	A			NT	'15-'16	€202,000	€202,000	
3.225	2041.09.16	S			NT	2021	NZ$128,000	NZ$128,000	
3.450	2043.12.01	S		013051DK0	NT	'13-'15	$2,500,000	$2,500,000	
1.150	2043.12.01	A			NT	'16-'17	€435,000	€435,000	
0.925	2045.05.08	A			NT	2020	€70,000	€70,000	
2.473	2046.02.16	S			MN	2021	A$100,000	A$100,000	
3.300	2046.12.01	S		013051DS3	BD	'15-'17	$5,200,000	$5,200,000	
3.050	2048.12.01	S		013051DY0	NT	'17-'18	$6,900,000	$6,900,000	
1.413	2050.03.31	A			MN	2020	€30,000	€30,000	
1.500	2050.04.07	A			MN	2020	€90,000	€90,000	
3.100	2050.06.01	S		013051ED5	NT	'18-'21	$8,920,000	$8,920,000	
2.070	2050.12.09	S		013051EN3	NT	2020	US$39,650	US$39,650	
2.950	2052.06.01	S		013051EQ6	BD	'21-'22	$3,500,000	$3,500,000	
4.450	2054.12.01	S		013051ES2	DB	'23-'24	$1,350,000	$1,350,000	
2.400	2060.06.01	S		01306ZDJ7	MN	2020	$200,000	$200,000	
2.850	2071.06.01	S		01306ZDK4	MN	2021	$125,000	$125,000	
3.060	2120.06.01	S		013051EJ2	MN	2020	$700,000	$700,000	

GUARANTEED DEBT
March 31, 2024

Cpn %	Maturity	Freq	Series	CUSIP	Type	Year	Issued Amount (000)	Outstanding Amount (000)	Ref. Note
ALBERTA CAPITAL FINANCE AUTHORITY									
4.450	2025.12.15	S	DX	01285PBU1	NT	2005	$300,000	$300,000	

British Columbia

Premier: David Eby (New Democratic Party)
Capital City: Victoria
Area: 994,735 sq. kilometres

Visit these Web sites:
 Province of British Columbia: www.gov.bc.ca
 British Columbia Investment Management Corporation: www.bci.ca

DBRS Bond Rating at April 30, 2024 ... AA high

	2023	2022
Employed	2,837,900	2,763,000
Unemployment rate (%)	5.5	4.1
Average weekly earnings (Dec.)	$1,230.39	$1,153.32
Building permits	$22,798,443,000	$25,809,451,000
Retail sales	$108,967,837,000	$101,201,717,000
Population (est. July 1)	5,519,013	5,319,324
December consumer price index (2002=100)	152.1	147.1
Sales tax (GST)	5%	5%
(PST)	7%	7%

DIRECT DEBT
March 31, 2024

Cpn %	Maturity	Freq	Series	CUSIP	Type	Year	Issued Amount (000)	Outstanding Amount (000)	Ref. Note
PROVINCE OF BRITISH COLUMBIA									
9.000	2024.08.23	S	BCCD-T	110709DP4	BD	1994	$400,000	$400,000	
9.000	2024.08.23	S	BCMTN-40	11070ZAW4	MN	1995	$35,000	$35,000	
9.000	2024.08.23	S	BCMTN-52	11070ZBJ2	MN	1995	$200,000	$200,000	
8.500	2024.08.23	S	BCMTN-56	11070ZBN3	MN	1995	$30,000	$30,000	
7.875	2024.08.23	S	BCMTN-62	11070ZBU7	MN	1996	$200,000	$200,000	
7.000	2024.08.23	S	BCMTN-82	11070ZCR3	MN	1999	$55,000	$55,000	
1.750	2024.09.27	S	BCUSG-10	110709AD4	BD	2019	US$1,250,000	US$1,250,000	
4.250	2024.11.27	S	BCAUD-1		MN	2014	A$700,000	A$700,000	
2.850	2025.06.18	S	BCCD-34	11070TAF5	BD	'14-'20	$4,050,000	$4,050,000	
0.875	2025.10.08	A	BCEURO-2		BD	2015	€500,000	€500,000	
6.500	2026.01.15	S	BCUSD-2	110709DL3	BD	1996	US$500,000	US$500,000	1
2.250	2026.06.02	S	BCUSG-9	11070TAK4	BD	2016	US$750,000	US$750,000	
2.300	2026.06.18	S	BCCD-36	11070TAJ7	BD	'16-'17	$1,500,000	$1,500,000	
0.900	2026.07.20	S	BCUSG-12	110709AH5	BD	2021	US$2,500,000	US$2,500,000	
8.000	2026.09.09	S	BCMTN-63	11070ZBV5	MN	1996	$110,000	$110,000	
7.000	2026.12.04	S	BCMTN-64	11070ZBW3	MN	1996	$40,000	$40,000	
7.000	2026.12.04	S	BCMTN-74	11070ZCH5	MN	1999	$60,000	$60,000	
2.500	2027.02.26	S	BCAUD-2		NT	'16-'17	A$170,000	A$170,000	
7.500	2027.06.09	S	BCMTN-65	11070ZBX1	MN	1997	$50,000	$50,000	
2.550	2027.06.18	S	BCCD-37	11070TAL2	NT	'17-'20	$2,300,000	$2,300,000	
6.150	2027.11.19	S	BCCD-W	110709EJ7	BD	'97-'99	$500,000	$500,000	
5.620	2028.08.17	S	BCMTN-70	11070ZCC6	MN	1998	$200,000	$200,000	
4.800	2028.11.15	S	BCUSG-14	110709AJ1	BD	2023	US$2,000,000	US$2,000,000	
2.950	2028.12.18	S	BCCD-38	110709GH9	BD	'18-'19	$2,000,000	$2,000,000	
5.150	2029.06.18	S	BCCD-14	110709FP2	BD	'07-'13	$495,000	$495,000	
5.700	2029.06.18	S	BCCD-X	110709EK4	BD	'98-'99	$2,285,000	$2,285,000	
5.861	2029.06.18	S	BCMTN-83	11070ZCS1	MN	1999	$250,000	$250,000	
2.500	2030.04.18	A	BCSFR-7		MN	2010	SFr100,000	SFr100,000	
2.200	2030.06.18	S	BCCD-40	110709GK2	BD	'19-'21	$4,210,000	$4,210,000	
1.300	2031.01.29	S	BCUSG-11	110709AE2	BD	2021	US$1,750,000	US$1,750,000	
5.000	2031.06.18	S	BCCD-19	110709FV9	MN	'08-'13	$1,035,000	$1,035,000	
1.550	2031.06.18	S	BCCD-41	110709AF9	BD	'21-'22	$3,800,000	$3,800,000	
6.350	2031.06.18	S	BCCD-Z	110709EX6	BD	'00-'01	$1,400,000	$1,400,000	
2.500	2032.05.16	S	AUD-3		MN	2021	A$70,000	A$70,000	
3.200	2032.06.18	S	BCCD-43	110709GL0	NT	'22-'23	$2,500,000	$2,500,000	
0.700	2032.07.20	A	BCEURO-5		MN	2016	€250,000	€250,000	
2.600	2032.12.14	S	AUD-4		MN	2021	A$78,000	A$78,000	
3.550	2033.06.18	S	BCCD-45	110709GN6	DB	'23-'24	$3,000,000	$3,000,000	
4.200	2033.07.06	S	BCUSG-13	11070TAM0	BD	2023	US$2,250,000	US$2,250,000	
4.150	2034.06.18	S	BCCD-46	110709AK8	BD	2024	$2,000,000	$2,600,000	
3.000	2034.07.24	A	BCEURO-17		BD	2024	€1,250,000	€1,250,000	
5.400	2035.06.18	S	BCCD-7	110709FJ6	BD	2004	$500,000	$500,000	
7.250	2036.09.01	S	BCUSD-3	110709EC2	BD	1996	US$300,000	US$300,000	1
1.337	2037.01.27	A	BCEURO-6		MN	2017	€150,000	€150,000	
4.700	2037.06.18	S	BCCD-11	110709FL1	BD	'06-'08	$1,500,000	$1,500,000	
3.210	2038.11.08	A	BCEURO-1		MN	2011	€40,000	€40,000	

Cpn %	Maturity	Freq	Series	CUSIP	Type	Year	Issued Amount (000)	Outstanding Amount (000)	Ref. Note
5.750	2039.01.09	S	BCMTN-69	11070ZCB8	MN	1998	$150,000	$150,000	
6.000	2039.01.09	S	BCMTN-73	11070ZCF9	MN	1998	$65,000	$65,000	
3.741	2039.04.01	A	BCEURO-16		NT	2023	€100,000	€100,000	
3.508	2039.06.07	A	EURO-14		NT	2023	€86,000	€86,000	
2.060	2039.06.09	A	BCEURO-13		MN	2022	€100,000	€100,000	
6.300	2039.08.23	S	BCMTN-84	11070ZCT9	MN	1999	$200,000	$200,000	
4.950	2040.06.18	S	BCCD-22	110709FY3	BD	'08-'10	$2,300,000	$2,300,000	
1.678	2040.12.18	A	BCEURO-3		NT	2015	€75,000	€75,000	
4.300	2042.06.18	S	BCCD-25	1107098Y1	BD	'10-'12	$3,850,000	$3,850,000	
0.590	2042.12.22	A	BCEURO-12		MN	2021	€135,000	€135,000	
1.250	2043.06.17	A	BCEURO-4		MN	2016	€100,000	€100,000	
5.250	2043.06.18	S	BCCD-1	11070ZDD3	MN	2003	$150,000	$150,000	
1.227	2044.04.25	A	BCEURO-7		MN	2019	€130,000	€130,000	
3.200	2044.06.18	S	BCCD-29	110709GC0	DB	'12-'14	$4,100,000	$4,100,000	
5.750	2044.08.23	S	BCCD-10	11070ZDL5	MN	'04-'08	$136,000	$136,000	
4.600	2045.06.18	S	BCCD-18	110709FU1	MN	2008	$50,000	$50,000	
1.000	2048.04.09	A	BCEURO-11		BD	2020	€170,000	€170,000	
4.900	2048.06.18	S	BCCD-15	110709FQ0	BD	'07-'11	$555,000	$555,000	
2.800	2048.06.18	S	BCCD-35	11070TAG3	BD	'15-'18	$5,000,000	$5,000,000	
0.478	2049.10.18	A	BCEURO-9		NT	'19-'23	€709,000	€709,000	
0.270	2050.03.30	A	BCEURO-10		NT	2020	€150,000	€150,000	
2.950	2050.06.18	S	BCCD-39	110709GJ5	NT	'18-'21	$6,400,000	$6,400,000	
2.750	2052.06.18	S	BCCD-42	110709AG7	BD	'21-'22	$4,300,000	$4,300,000	
3.402	2053.06.05	A	BCEURO-15		NT	2023	€80,000	€80,000	
4.250	2053.12.18	S	BCCD-44	110709GM8	BD	'22-'24	$3,800,000	$4,800,000	
3.500	2055.06.18	S	BCCD-27	110709GA4	MN	'12-'13	$190,000	$190,000	
3.300	2062.06.18	S	BCCD-30	11070TAD0	BD	2013	$230,500	$230,500	

GUARANTEED DEBT
March 31, 2024

Cpn %	Maturity	Freq	Series	CUSIP	Type	Year	Issued Amount (000)	Outstanding Amount (000)	Ref. Note
BRITISH COLUMBIA INVESTMENT MANAGEMENT CORPORATION									
4.900	2033.06.02	S	1	110610AA0	NT	'23-'24	$2,250,000	$2,250,000	

REFERENCES
1. Callable if taxation laws requiring additional payments are imposed or levied.

Manitoba

Premier: Wab Kinew (New Democratic Party)
Capital City: Winnipeg
Area: 647,797 sq. kilometres

Visit this Web site:
Province of Manitoba: www.gov.mb.ca

DBRS Bond Rating at November 3, 2023 ... A high

	2023	2022
Employed	703,100	682,400
Unemployment rate (%)	4.2	4.3
Average weekly earnings (Dec.)	$1,115.59	$1,073.01
Building permits	$3,887,563,000	$3,772,470,000
Retail sales	$26,958,089,000	$25,577,616,000
Population (est. July 1)	1,454,902	1,409,223
December consumer price index (2002=100)	158.2	155.5
Sales tax (GST)	5%	5%
(PST)	7%	7%

FP Bonds — Government 2024

DIRECT DEBT
March 31, 2024

Cpn %	Maturity	Freq	Series	CUSIP	Type	Year	Issued Amount (000)	Outstanding Amount (000)	Ref. Note
PROVINCE OF MANITOBA									
2.600	2024.04.16	S	GX	563469UU7	DB	2019	US$1,000,000	US$1,000,000	
3.050	2024.05.14	S	GI	563469UD5	DB	2014	US$800,000	US$800,000	
3.300	2024.06.02	S	GH	563469UC7	DB	2014	$900,000	$900,000	
4.800	2024.06.30	S	C086	56344ZLV9	MN	2006	$50,000	$50,000	1
4.250	2025.03.03	S	C140		NT	'14-'15	A$375,000	A$375,000	
2.450	2025.06.02	S	GJ	563469UE3	DB	'15-'20	$2,950,000	$2,950,000	
4.400	2025.09.05	S	C119	56344ZPH6	DB	'10-'13	$715,000	$715,000	
7.750	2025.12.22	S	DT	563469DS1	DB	1995	$300,000	$300,000	2
0.200	2026.04.20	A			NT	2020	SFr100,000	SFr100,000	
2.550	2026.06.02	S	GN	563469UJ2	DB	'16-'17	$1,900,000	$1,900,000	
3.750	2026.06.09	S	C145		NT	'15-'16	A$290,000	A$290,000	
2.125	2026.06.22	S	GP	563469UL7	DB	2016	US$500,000	US$500,000	
2.600	2027.06.02	S	GS	563469UP8	DB	'17-'18	$1,500,000	$1,500,000	
3.600	2027.08.17	S	C157		MN	'17-'18	A$300,000	A$300,000	
3.000	2028.06.02	S		563469UR4	DB	'18-'23	$2,050,000	$2,050,000	
3.500	2028.08.22	S	C161		MN	'18-'19	A$225,000	A$225,000	
1.500	2028.10.25	S	HB	563469UY9	DB	2021	US$1,000,000	US$1,000,000	
2.570	2028.11.28	A	C155		MN	2016	HK$1,070,000	HK$1,070,000	
0.250	2029.03.15	A			NT	2019	SFr250,000	SFr250,000	
2.915	2029.04.10	S	C169		NT	2019	NZ$39,500	NZ$39,500	
2.750	2029.06.02	S		563469UT0	DB	'19-'23	$1,800,000	$1,800,000	
3.250	2029.09.05	S	C136	56344ZQC6	MN	'13-'16	$456,000	$456,000	
5.550	2029.12.03	S	C074	56344ZJD2	MN	2004	$100,000	$100,000	3
2.050	2030.06.02	S		563469UV5	DB	'20-'21	$1,300,000	$1,300,000	
10.500	2031.03.05	S	CL	563469CX1	DB	1990	$599,945	$599,945	4
6.300	2031.03.05	S	D025	56344ZCG2	MN	'00-'10	$410,000	$410,000	
4.875	2031.03.05	S	D129	56344ZKL2	MN	2005	$100,000	$100,000	5
2.050	2031.06.02	S		563469UX1	NT	'21-'22	$1,900,000	$1,900,000	
2.750	2032.02.03	S			MN	2022	A$36,000	A$36,000	
6.300	2032.07.26	S	C049	56344ZEH8	MN	2002	$50,000	$50,000	6
6.300	2032.10.29	S	C052	56344ZEW5	MN	2002	$30,000	$30,000	7
3.900	2032.12.02	S		563469VA0	NT	'22-'23	$1,650,000	$1,650,000	
2.850	2033.02.03	S			MN	2022	A$36,000	A$36,000	
3.800	2033.06.02	S		563469VB8	DB	'23-'24	$1,500,000	$1,500,000	
4.300	2033.07.27	S	HF	563469VC6	DB	2023	US$1,000,000	US$1,000,000	
3.750	2033.09.05	S	C141	56344ZQF9	MN	2014	$130,000	$130,000	
4.250	2034.06.02	S		563469VE2	DB	2024	$300,000	$900,000	
1.252	2034.07.18	A			MN	2019	SKr500,000	SKr500,000	
5.330	2035.01.19	S	C076	56344ZJM2	MN	2005	$75,000	$75,000	8
0.600	2035.03.30	A			MN	2020	€60,000	€60,000	
1.390	2035.06.11	A	C142		NT	2015	€32,000	€32,000	9
2.000	2036.12.01	S	C087	56344ZLW7	MN	2006	$100,000	$100,000	
0.750	2037.02.02	A			MN	2022	€70,000	€70,000	
3.740	2037.02.16	A			MN	2022	NZ$130,000	NZ$130,000	
5.700	2037.03.05	S	FA	563469EZ4	DB	'04-'06	$700,000	$700,000	
4.600	2038.03.05	S	PB	563469FL4	DB	2007	$950,000	$950,000	

FP Bonds — Government 2024

Cpn %	Maturity	Freq	Series	CUSIP	Type	Year	Issued Amount (000)	Outstanding Amount (000)	Ref. Note
4.250	2039.03.05	S	C124	56344ZPN3	MN	2011	$210,000	$210,000	
0.800	2039.03.15	A			MN	2019	SFr150,000	SFr150,000	
1.000	2039.06.25	A	C154		MN	2016	€40,000	€40,000	
4.650	2039.07.16	S	C091	56344ZME6	MN	2007	$100,000	$100,000	10
6.200	2040.03.05	S	C031	56344ZCK3	MN	'00-'01	$276,000	$276,000	
4.650	2040.03.05	S	FK	563469FQ3	DB	'08-'10	$800,000	$800,000	
0.700	2040.04.20	A			NT	2020	SFr100,000	SFr100,000	
1.770	2040.06.25	A	C143		NT	'15-'16	€470,000	€470,000	
1.740	2041.02.25	A	C147		NT	2016	€85,000	€85,000	
4.100	2041.03.05	S	FR	563469TM7	DB	'10-'15	$1,300,000	$1,300,000	
1.500	2041.06.25	A	C151		MN	'16-'19	€285,000	€285,000	
1.950	2041.06.25	A	H062		MN	2016	€45,000	€45,000	
0.700	2041.11.25	A			MN	2021	€160,000	€160,000	
6.000	2042.03.05	S	C040	56344ZDP1	MN	2002	$350,000	$350,000	
4.400	2042.03.05	S	FT	563469TQ8	DB	2011	$400,000	$400,000	
3.350	2043.03.05	S	GA	563469TW5	DB	'12-'13	$550,000	$550,000	
5.800	2044.03.05	S	C068	56344ZHN2	MN	'04-'06	$120,000	$120,000	
5.000	2044.09.05	S	C092	56344ZMF3	MN	'07-'11	$157,035	$157,035	
4.050	2045.09.05	S	GG	563469UB9	DB	'13-'14	$1,500,000	$1,500,000	
0.800	2046.04.27	S	C149		NT	2016	Jp¥5,000,000	Jp¥5,000,000	
0.700	2046.08.30	S	C153		MN	2016	Jp¥6,000,000	Jp¥6,000,000	
2.850	2046.09.05	S	GK	563469UF0	DB	'15-'16	$1,950,000	$1,950,000	
0.700	2046.12.05	S	C156		MN	2016	Jp¥5,000,000	Jp¥5,000,000	
3.400	2048.09.05	S	GR	563469UN3	DB	'17-'18	$2,100,000	$2,100,000	
1.500	2049.06.25	A	C170		NT	2019	€100,000	€100,000	
1.250	2049.06.25	A	C176		NT	2020	€75,000	€75,000	
0.475	2049.11.02	A			NT	2020	€100,000	€100,000	
4.700	2050.03.05	S	FN	563469TH8	DB	'09-'12	$350,000	$350,000	
3.200	2050.03.05	S	GV	563469US2	DB	'18-'20	$2,550,000	$2,550,000	
2.050	2052.09.05	S		563469UW3	DB	'20-'21	$1,800,000	$1,800,000	
3.150	2052.09.05	S	C129	56344ZPV5	MN	'12-'14	$610,000	$610,000	
3.800	2053.09.05	S		563469UZ6	DB	'22-'23	$1,900,000	$1,900,000	
3.650	2054.09.05	S	C139	56344ZQG7	MN	2014	$75,000	$75,000	
4.400	2055.09.05	S		563469VD4	NT	2024	$1,100,000	$1,400,000	
5.200	2060.03.05	S	C110	56344ZNV7	MN	'09-'12	$325,000	$325,000	
4.625	2063.03.05	S	C109	56344ZNU9	MN	'09-'15	$255,000	$255,000	
3.450	2063.03.05	S	C137	56344ZQE2	MN	'13-'17	$1,199,000	$1,199,000	
3.100	2068.03.05	S	C160	56344ZQJ1	MN	'18-'24	$2,015,000	$2,015,000	
2.950	2120.09.05	S		56344ZQM4	MN	2020	$600,000	$600,000	

REFERENCES
1. Extendible semiannually to June 30, 2036 at an interest rate of 4.8%.
2. Issued on behalf of Manitoba Hydro.
3. Extendible at the option of the holder to Dec. 3, 2029 with an interest rate of 5.55%.
4. Of the total, $299,945,000 issued on the exercise of warrants attached to the initial $300,000,000 issue.
5. Extendible to Mar. 5, 2031 with an interest rate of 4.875%.
6. Extendible to July 26, 2032 with an interest rate of 6.3%.
7. Extendible to Oct. 29, 2032 with an interest rate of 6.3%.
8. Extendible to Jan. 19, 2035 with an interest rate of 5.33%.
9. Redeem. at par in whole but not in part once on June 11, 2025 upon 5 business days' notice.
10. Puttable at par at the holder's option effective July 16, 2018.

New Brunswick

Premier: Blaine Higgs (Progressive Conservative)
Capital City: Fredericton
Area: 72,908 sq. kilometres

Visit this Web site:
  Province of New Brunswick: www.gnb.ca

DBRS Bond Rating at May 27, 2024 ... A high

	2023	2022
Employed	390,800	379,100
Unemployment rate (%)	6.3	7.8
Average weekly earnings (Dec.)	$1,116.94	$1,077.7
Building permits	$1,741,251,000	$1,699,145,000
Retail sales	$17,224,115,000	$16,287,088,000
Population (est. July 1)	834,691	812,061
December consumer price index (2002=100)	157.8	153.4
Sales tax (HST)	15%	15%

DIRECT DEBT
March 31, 2024

PROVINCE OF NEW BRUNSWICK

Cpn %	Maturity	Freq	Series	CUSIP	Type	Year	Issued Amount (000)	Outstanding Amount (000)	Ref. Note
3.650	2024.06.03	S	HN	642869AJ0	DB	'13-'15	$850,000	$850,000	
1.800	2025.08.14	S	IF	642866GR2	BD	'20-'22	$1,000,000	$1,000,000	
2.600	2026.08.14	S	HS	642866GK7	DB	'16-'21	$1,000,000	$1,000,000	
2.350	2027.08.14	S	HX	642866GM3	DB	'17-'18	$1,000,000	$1,000,000	
3.625	2028.05.15	S	HW	642869AM3	BD	2018	US$500,000	US$500,000	
3.100	2028.08.14	S	HZ	642866GN1	DB	'18-'22	$1,200,000	$1,200,000	
5.650	2028.12.27	S	FT	642866ET0	DB	'98-'99	$500,000	$500,000	
0.250	2029.01.19	A	HV		NT	'17-'18	SFr300,000	SFr300,000	
6.290	2029.12.15	S	FV	642866EW3	DB	1999	$50,000	$50,000	1
2.550	2031.08.14	S	II	642866GT8	NT	2022	$600,000	$600,000	
0.200	2031.11.07	A	HU		NT	2016	SFr400,000	SFr400,000	
3.950	2032.08.14	S	IJ	642866HA8	DB	'22-'23	$1,200,000	$1,200,000	
0.125	2032.12.06	A	IE		NT	2019	SFr100,000	SFr100,000	
4.450	2033.08.14	S	IK	642866HB6	DB	'23-'24	$900,000	$900,000	
5.500	2034.01.27	S	GJ	642866FR3	DB	2004	$550,000	$550,000	
4.650	2035.09.26	S	GO	642866FW2	DB	'05-'07	$650,000	$650,000	2
4.550	2037.03.26	S	GS	642866FZ5	DB	2007	$900,000	$900,000	2
4.800	2039.09.26	S	GT	642866GA9	DB	'07-'10	$1,200,000	$1,200,000	
0.250	2039.12.06	A	ID		NT	2019	SFr125,000	SFr125,000	
4.800	2041.06.03	S	HB	642869AA9	DB	'10-'14	$1,175,000	$1,175,000	
3.550	2043.06.03	S	HH	642869AE1	DB	'12-'14	$1,200,000	$1,200,000	
3.800	2045.08.14	S	HO	642866GG6	DB	'14-'15	$1,250,000	$1,250,000	
3.100	2048.08.14	S	HT	642866GL5	BD	'16-'18	$1,150,000	$1,150,000	
3.050	2050.08.14	S	IC	642866GQ4	DB	'19-'20	$1,500,000	$1,500,000	
2.900	2052.08.14	S	IH	642866GS0	DB	'21-'23	$600,000	$600,000	
5.000	2054.08.14	S	IL	642866HC4	NT	'23-'24	$600,000	$900,000	
3.550	2055.06.03	S	HG	642866GE1	NT	2012	$315,000	$315,000	
3.550	2065.06.03	S	HK	642866GF8	MN	'13-'19	$585,000	$585,000	

GUARANTEED DEBT
March 31, 2024

Cpn %	Maturity	Freq	Series	CUSIP	Type	Year	Issued Amount (000)	Outstanding Amount (000)	Ref. Note

NEW BRUNSWICK MUNICIPAL FINANCE CORPORATION

Cpn %	Maturity	Freq	Series	CUSIP	Type	Year	Issued Amount (000)	Outstanding Amount (000)	Ref. Note
Var.	2014.06.14-2033	S	BI		SB	2013	$73,647	$24,279	
Var.	2014.11.20-2033	S	BJ		SB	2013	$52,370	$14,395	
Var.	2015.05.15-2034	S	BK		SB	2014	$47,517	$11,238	
Var.	2015.12.08-2034	S	BL		SB	2014	$80,661	$29,258	

REFERENCES
1. Was puttable at par on Dec. 15, 2007 at the option of the noteholder. Prior to Dec. 15, 2007, the interest rate was 5.75%.

2. Proceeds from these issues split between Province of New Brunswick and New Brunswick Power; each pay 1.5% and 1%, respectively, on their share of the proceeds.

Newfoundland and Labrador

Premier: Andrew Furey (Liberal)
Capital City: St John's
Area: 405,212 sq. kilometres

Visit these Web sites:
    Province of Newfoundland and Labrador: www.gov.nf.ca
    Newfoundland and Labrador Hydro: nlhydro.com

DBRS Bond Rating at August 17, 2023 ... A

	2023	2022
Employed	238,000	236,800
Unemployment rate (%)	10.5	10.1
Average weekly earnings (Dec.)	$1,229.55	$1,176.83
Building permits	$474,994,000	$546,850,000
Retail sales	$11,414,146,000	$10,930,724,000
Population (est. July 1)	538,605	525,972
December consumer price index (2002=100)	159.8	154.6
Sales tax (HST)	15%	15%

DIRECT DEBT
March 31, 2024

Cpn %	Maturity	Freq	Series	CUSIP	Type	Year	Issued Amount (000)	Outstanding Amount (000)	Ref. Note
PROVINCE OF NEWFOUNDLAND AND LABRADOR									
2.300	2025.06.02	S	6W	651333FS0	DB	'15-'20	$1,050,000	$1,050,000	
9.150	2025.07.07	S	6B	651333EA0	DB	1995	$100,000	$100,000	
8.450	2026.02.05	S	6C	651333EB8	DB	1996	$150,000	$150,000	
3.000	2026.06.02	S	6Z	651333FV3	DB	2016	$1,000,000	$1,000,000	
1.250	2027.06.02	S	7J	651333GF7	DB	2020	$500,000	$500,000	
3.850	2027.10.17	S	7M	651333GK6	DB	'22-'23	$1,400,000	$1,400,000	
6.150	2028.04.17	S	6F	651333EE2	DB	1998	$450,000	$450,000	
2.850	2028.06.02	S	7D	651333FZ4	BD	'17-'22	$1,250,000	$1,250,000	
2.850	2029.06.02	S	7G	651333GC4	DB	'19-'20	$1,000,000	$1,000,000	
6.500	2029.10.17	S	6H	651333EG7	DB	1999	$200,000	$200,000	
1.750	2030.06.02	S	7I	651333GE0	DB	'20-'21	$1,000,000	$1,000,000	
6.550	2030.10.17	S	6K	651333EZ5	DB	2000	$450,000	$450,000	
2.050	2031.06.02	S	7K	651333GG5	DB	'21-'22	$900,000	$900,000	
4.150	2033.06.02	S	7O	651333GM2	DB	'23-'24	$900,000	$900,000	
5.600	2033.10.17	S	6R	651333FM3	DB	2003	$300,000	$300,000	
5.700	2035.10.17	S	6T	651333FP6	DB	2004	$300,000	$300,000	
4.500	2037.04.17	S	6U	651333FQ4	DB	2006	$350,000	$350,000	
4.650	2040.10.17	S	6V	651333FR2	DB	2007	$650,000	$650,000	
6.240	2042.10.17	S	6Q	651333FK7	DB	2002	$250,000	$250,000	
3.300	2046.10.17	S	6X	651333FT8	DB	'15-'16	$2,050,000	$2,050,000	
3.700	2048.10.17	S	7C	651333FY7	DB	'16-'19	$1,350,000	$1,350,000	
2.650	2050.10.17	S	7H	651333GD2	DB	'19-'21	$1,900,000	$1,900,000	
3.150	2052.12.02	S	7L	651333GH3	DB	'21-'22	$750,000	$750,000	
4.100	2054.10.17	S	7N	651333GL4	DB	'22-'24	$900,000	$900,000	

GUARANTEED DEBT
March 31, 2024

Cpn %	Maturity	Freq	Series	CUSIP	Type	Year	Issued Amount (000)	Outstanding Amount (000)	Ref. Note
LABRADOR ISLAND LINK FUNDING TRUST									
3.760	2033.06.01	S	A	505443AA9	BD	2013	$725,000	$725,000	
3.860	2045.12.01	S	B	505443AB7	BD	2013	$600,000	$600,000	
3.850	2053.12.01	S	C	505443AC5	BD	2013	$1,075,000	$1,075,000	
Var.	2020.12.01-2057	S			SB	2017	$1,050,000	$976,500	
MUSKRAT FALLS/LABRADOR TRANSMISSION ASSETS FUNDING TRUST									
3.630	2029.06.01	S	A	628153AA6	BD	2013	$650,000	$650,000	
3.830	2037.06.01	S	B	628153AB4	BD	2013	$675,000	$675,000	
3.860	2048.12.01	S	C	628153AC2	BD	2013	$1,275,000	$1,275,000	
Var.	2020.12.01-2052	S			SB	2017	$1,850,000	$1,708,220	
Var.	2037.12.01-2057				SB	2022	$1,000,000	$1,000,000	

FP Bonds — Government 2024

Cpn %	Maturity	Freq	Series	CUSIP	Type	Year	Issued Amount (000)	Outstanding Amount (000)	Ref. Note
NEWFOUNDLAND AND LABRADOR HYDRO									
8.400	2026.02.27	S	Y	651329AW4	DB	1996	$300,000	$300,000	
6.650	2031.08.27	S	AB	651329BA1	DB	'01-'02	$300,000	$300,000	
5.700	2033.07.14	S	AD	651329BC7	DB	2003	$125,000	$125,000	
3.600	2045.12.01	S	AF	651329BE3	DB	'14-'17	$500,000	$500,000	

Provinces

Nova Scotia

Premier: Tim Houston (Progressive Conservative)
Capital City: Halifax
Area: 55,284 sq. kilometres

Visit this Web site:
Province of Nova Scotia: www.novascotia.ca

DBRS Bond Rating at November 9, 2023 ... A high

	2023	2022
Employed	507,900	492,200
Unemployment rate (%)	5.9	6.2
Average weekly earnings (Dec.)	$1,084.13	$1,033.77
Building permits	$2,883,618,000	$2,610,681,000
Retail sales	$21,205,457,000	$19,754,448,000
Population (est. July 1)	1,058,694	1,019,725
December consumer price index (2002=100)	162.1	156.4
Sales tax (HST)	15%	15%

DIRECT DEBT
March 31, 2024

Cpn %	Maturity	Freq	Series	CUSIP	Type	Year	Issued Amount (000)	Outstanding Amount (000)	Ref. Note
PROVINCE OF NOVA SCOTIA									
F.R.	2024.11.09	Q	P122	66989ZES3	MN	'17-'19	$767,500	$767,500	
1.350	2025.04.21	S	P126	66989ZEW4	NT	2020	$535,000	$535,000	
2.150	2025.06.01	S	D8	669827BG1	BD	2015	$300,000	$300,000	
6.600	2027.06.01	S	9Z	669827EB9	BD	'97-'98	$550,000	$550,000	
2.100	2027.06.01	S	D9	669827GA9	BD	2016	$650,000	$650,000	
1.100	2028.06.01	S	E3	669827GD3	BD	'21-'23	$1,100,000	$1,100,000	
F.R.	2029.05.09	Q		669827GJ0	NT	2024	$500,000	$500,000	
4.050	2029.06.01	S	E5	669827GF8	DB	2023	$600,000	$600,000	
2.000	2030.09.01	S	E2	669827GC5	DB	'20-'21	$1,200,000	$1,200,000	
6.600	2031.12.01	S	B2	669827EW3	BD	2001	$300,000	$300,000	
2.400	2031.12.01	S	E4	669827GE1	BD	'21-'22	$900,000	$900,000	
4.050	2033.06.01	S		669827GG6	DB	2023	$600,000	$600,000	
5.800	2033.06.01	S	B5	669827FL6	BD	'03-'04	$600,000	$600,000	
4.900	2035.06.01	S	B7	669827FP7	DB	2005	$350,000	$350,000	
4.500	2037.06.01	S	B8	669827FQ5	BD	'06-'08	$750,000	$750,000	
4.700	2041.06.01	S	D3	669827FW2	BD	'09-'10	$950,000	$950,000	
4.400	2042.06.01	S	D6	6698278Z3	DB	'11-'12	$1,050,000	$1,050,000	
3.450	2045.06.01	S	D7	669827FZ5	DB	'14-'15	$325,000	$325,000	
3.150	2051.12.01	S	E1	669827GB7	DB	'19-'21	$2,000,000	$2,000,000	
4.750	2054.12.01	S		669827GH4	NT	2023	$600,000	$1,100,000	
3.500	2062.06.02	S	P112	66989ZEG9	MN	'12-'13	$1,488,800	$1,488,800	

GUARANTEED DEBT
March 31, 2024

Cpn %	Maturity	Freq	Series	CUSIP	Type	Year	Issued Amount (000)	Outstanding Amount (000)	Ref. Note
NOVA SCOTIA POWER FINANCE CORPORATION									
11.000	2031.02.26	S	AM	669812BP3	NT	1991	$200,000	$200,000	

Ontario

Premier: Doug Ford (Progressive Conservative)
Capital City: Toronto
Area: 1,076,395 sq. kilometres

Visit these Web sites:
    Province of Ontario: www.ontario.ca
    Ontario Electricity Financial Corporation: www.oefc.on.ca

DBRS Bond Rating at December 7, 2023 ... AA low

	2023	2022
Employed	7,913,900	7,786,900
Unemployment rate (%)	6.3	5.3
Average weekly earnings (Dec.)	$1,238.15	$1,197.94
Building permits	$56,188,581,000	$55,269,414,000
Retail sales	$297,331,543,000	$271,923,767,000
Population (est. July 1)	15,608,369	15,109,416
December consumer price index (2002=100)	160	154.8
Sales tax (HST)	13%	13%

FP Bonds — Government 2024

DIRECT DEBT
March 31, 2024

Cpn %	Maturity	Freq	Series	CUSIP	Type	Year	Issued Amount (000)	Outstanding Amount (000)	Ref. Note
PROVINCE OF ONTARIO									
3.200	2024.05.16	S	G66	68323ACT9	BD	2014	US$1,250,000	US$1,250,000	
1.875	2024.05.21	A	EMTN110		MN	2014	€1,750,000	€1,750,000	
3.500	2024.06.02	S	DMTN223	68323ACG7	MN	'13-'14	$11,550,000	$6,350,000	1
0.375	2024.06.14	A	EMTN114		NT	2017	€1,500,000	€1,500,000	
3.100	2024.06.21	A	14A	68323ACR3	SV	2014		$17,288	
3.100	2024.06.21		14C	68323ACS1	SV	2014		$8,620	2
4.250	2024.08.22	S	ADI3		BD	2014	A$350,000	A$350,000	
2.300	2024.09.08	S	DMTN241	68333ZAF4	BD	'19-'21	$3,500,000	$3,500,000	
0.875	2025.01.21	A	EMTN111		MN	2015	€1,250,000	€1,250,000	1
2.650	2025.02.05	S	G77	68323AER1	BD	'18-'19	$2,700,000	$2,700,000	3
0.625	2025.04.17	A	EMTN116		BD	2018	€1,500,000	€1,500,000	
2.600	2025.06.02	S	DMTN227	68323ACX0	BD	2015	$13,600,000	$13,600,000	1
9.500	2025.06.02	S	JE	683234JA7	BD	1994	$500,000	$460,000	
2.350	2025.06.21	A	15A	68323ADG6	SV	2015		$3,308	
2.350	2025.06.21		15C	68323ADD3	SV	2015		$2,616	2
3.100	2025.08.26	S	ADI4		BD	'15-'16	A$365,000	A$365,000	
1.750	2025.09.08	S	DMTN245	68333ZAK3	BD	2020	$9,050,000	$9,050,000	
8.500	2025.12.02	S	JQ	683234JQ2	BD	1995	$1,000,000	$1,000,000	
0.625	2026.01.21	S	G87	683234AS7	BD	2021	US$3,500,000	US$3,500,000	
8.000	2026.02.06	S	JY	683234JV1	BD	1996	$50,000	$12,500	
1.050	2026.04.14	S	G89	683234AT5	BD	2021	US$3,000,000	US$3,000,000	
2.500	2026.04.27	S	G69	68323ADP6	BD	2016	US$1,000,000	US$1,000,000	
2.250	2026.05.26	A	EMTN126		BD	2022	£500,000	£500,000	
2.400	2026.06.02	S	DMTN229	68323ADM3	BD	2016	$7,500,000	$7,500,000	
8.000	2026.06.02	S	JU	683234JT6	BD	'95-'96	$1,000,000	$1,000,000	
2.300	2026.06.15	S	G83	68323AFF6	BD	2019	US$1,750,000	US$1,750,000	
2.200	2026.06.21	A	16A	68323ADT8	SV	2016		$6,087	
2.200	2026.06.21		16C	68323ADU5	SV	2016		$4,945	2
1.350	2026.09.08	S	DMTN250	68333ZAQ0	BD	'21-'22	$2,000,000	$2,000,000	
8.000	2026.12.02	S	KR	683234KN7	BD	'97-'98	$425,000	$386,500	4
7.000	2026.12.02	S	MH	683234MK1	BD	1999	$124,584	$124,584	5
0.250	2026.12.15	A	EMTN121		BD	2021	£1,750,000	£1,750,000	
3.500	2027.01.27	S	ADI5		BD	2017	A$315,000	A$315,000	
1.850	2027.02.01	S	DMTN244	68333ZAJ6	BD	'20-'21	$3,250,000	$3,250,000	3
7.500	2027.02.03	S	KN	683234KJ6	BD	1997	$300,000	$58,220	
6.950	2027.02.03	S	KT	683234KQ0	MN	1997	$200,000	$8,726	
7.500	2027.02.03	S	KY	683234KS6	BD	1997	$68,000	$11,549	6
7.500	2027.02.03	S	LA	683234LA4	BD	1997	$50,000	$5,507	
7.375	2027.02.04	S	KQ	683234KM9	BD	1998	$125,000	$990	7
0.375	2027.04.08	A	EMTN117		BD	2020	€1,000,000	€1,000,000	
3.100	2027.05.19	S	G92	683234DB1	BD	2022	US$2,250,000	US$2,250,000	
1.050	2027.05.21	S	G85	683234AQ1	BD	2020	US$1,750,000	US$1,750,000	
2.600	2027.06.02	S	DMTN234	68323AEE0	BD	'17-'20	$8,400,000	$8,400,000	
7.600	2027.06.02	S	KJ	683234KG2	BD	'96-'04	$4,835,200	$4,835,200	1
2.150	2027.06.21	A	17A	68323AEN0	SV	2017		$4,073	
2.150	2027.06.21		17C	68323AEJ9	SV	2017		$2,679	2

FP Bonds — Government 2024

Cpn %	Maturity	Freq	Series	CUSIP	Type	Year	Issued Amount (000)	Outstanding Amount (000)	Ref. Note
1.050	2027.09.08	S	DMTN247	68333ZAM9	BD	2020	$2,000,000	$2,000,000	
3.600	2028.03.08	S	DMTN256	68333ZAW7	DB	'22-'23	$5,500,000	$5,500,000	
2.900	2028.06.02	S	DMTN238	68333ZAC1	BD	'18-'19	$9,550,000	$9,550,000	
2.850	2028.06.21	A	18A	68323AEZ3	SV	2018		$734	
2.850	2028.06.21		18C	68323AFA7	SV	2018		$1,075	2
6.250	2028.08.25	S	LQ	683234LN6	BD	'98-'99	$723,843	$80,620	1
3.400	2028.09.08	S	DMTN259	68333ZAZ0	DB	2023	$2,000,000	$2,000,000	
3.200	2028.10.12	S	ADI6		BD	'18-'21	A$115,000	A$115,000	
F.R.	2028.11.27	Q		68333ZBB2	BD	2023	$2,600,000	$2,600,000	
4.200	2029.01.18	S	G93	683234DQ8	BD	2024	US$3,000,000	US$3,000,000	
6.500	2029.03.08	S	LK	683234LJ5	BD	'98-'04	$4,727,000	$4,727,000	
2.700	2029.06.02	S	DMTN240	68333ZAE7	BD	'19-'20	$9,325,000	$9,325,000	
0.250	2029.06.28	A	EMTN115		BD	2017	SFr400,000	SFr400,000	
2.000	2029.10.02	S	G84	68323AFG4	BD	2019	US$1,250,000	US$1,250,000	
2.700	2029.10.26		ADI7		MN	2019	A$40,000	A$40,000	
1.550	2029.11.01	S	DMTN251	68333ZAR8	MN	'21-'22	$5,500,000	$5,500,000	3
2.050	2030.06.02	S	DMTN243	68333ZAH0	BD	2020	$11,650,000	$11,650,000	
1.125	2030.10.07	S	G86	683234AR9	BD	2020	US$1,250,000	US$1,250,000	
0.010	2030.11.25	A	EMTN120		BD	2020	€2,500,000	€2,500,000	
1.350	2030.12.02	S	DMTN248	68333ZAN7	BD	'20-'21	$7,000,000	$7,000,000	
9.500	2031.01.13	S	JN	683234JN9	BD	1995	$125,000	$125,000	
1.600	2031.02.25	S	G88	68323AFH2	BD	2021	US$1,500,000	US$1,500,000	
5.200	2031.06.02	S	DMTN206	68323AAB0	MN	2010	$133,300	$133,300	
2.150	2031.06.02	S	DMTN249	68333ZAP2	DB	2021	$8,850,000	$8,850,000	
6.200	2031.06.02	S	NF	683234NM6	BD	'00-'02	$3,000,000	$3,000,000	
0.250	2031.06.09	A	EMTN123		BD	2021	€1,000,000	€1,000,000	
1.800	2031.10.14	S	G90	68323AFJ8	BD	2021	US$1,000,000	US$1,000,000	
2.250	2031.12.02	S	DMTN253	68333ZAT4	BD	'21-'22	$6,350,000	$6,350,000	
2.500	2031.12.10	S	ADI9		BD	2021	A$36,000	A$36,000	
2.125	2032.01.21	S	G91	683234AU2	BD	2022	US$1,500,000	US$1,500,000	
4.050	2032.02.02	S	DMTN257	68333ZAX5	BD	2023	$3,000,000	$3,000,000	3
3.750	2032.06.02	S	DMTN254	68333ZAU1	BD	'22-'23	$9,650,000	$9,650,000	
2.600	2032.12.10	S	ADI10		BD	2021	A$36,000	A$36,000	
4.100	2033.03.04	S		68333ZBD8	BD	2024	$1,500,000	$1,500,000	8
5.850	2033.03.08	S	DMTN110	683234VA3	MN	2004	$200,000	$188,000	9
5.850	2033.03.08	S	DMTN116	683234VP0	MN	2004	$100,000	$100,000	10
5.850	2033.03.08	S	DMTN61	683234SL3	BD	'03-'12	$4,674,610	$4,674,610	11
0.050	2033.05.12	A	EMTN122		BD	2021	SFr250,000	SFr250,000	
3.650	2033.06.02	S	DMTN258	68333ZAY3	BD	'23-'24	$12,950,000	$12,950,000	
3.100	2034.01.31	A	EMTN127		BD	2024	€1,250,000	€1,250,000	
4.150	2034.06.02	S		68333ZBC0	DB	2024	$3,250,000	$6,500,000	
5.000	2034.07.13	S	DMTN157	683234XT0	MN	2005	$47,500	$47,500	
9.400	2034.07.13	S	EMTN5		MN	1994	$300,000	$300,000	
2.000	2034.10.03	S	ADI8		NT	'19-'23	A$355,000	A$355,000	
9.750	2034.11.03	S	HY	683234HS0	BD	1994	$280,000	$248,800	
Z.R.	2035.01.10		HZ-JD	683234HV3	BD	1994	$230,800	$21,049	12
9.500	2035.01.12	S	JG	683234JC3	BD	2007	$132,950	$110,950	13
9.875	2035.02.08	S	JJ	683234HU5	BD	1995	$73,000	$32,000	
5.600	2035.06.02	S	DMTN119	683234VR6	DB	'04-'16	$7,556,209	$7,338,509	14
5.350	2035.06.02	S	DMTN133	683234WK0	MN	2005	$150,000	$150,000	15
8.250	2036.06.20	S	KC	683234KC1	BD	1996	$211,000	$98,984	

FP Bonds — Government 2024

Cpn %	Maturity	Freq	Series	CUSIP	Type	Year	Issued Amount (000)	Outstanding Amount (000)	Ref. Note
2.000	2036.12.01	S	DMTN158	683234XU7	BD	'05-'09	$2,844,000	$2,844,000	1,16
4.700	2037.06.02	S	DMTN164	683234YD4	MN	'06-'07	$9,100,000	$9,100,000	1
5.200	2037.12.20	S	DMTN138	683234WR5	MN	2005	$100,000	$100,000	
10.000	2038.06.02	S	DMTN117	683234VQ8	MN	2004	$75,000	$75,000	
8.100	2038.06.20	S	KG	683234KE7	BD	1996	$120,000	$120,000	
5.750	2038.07.13	S	LS	683234LW6	BD	1998	$50,000	$50,000	
6.000	2038.08.25	S	LT	683234LX4	BD	1998	$100,000	$86,500	
4.600	2039.06.02	S	DMTN182	683234ZP6	MN	'08-'10	$9,700,000	$9,700,000	1
5.650	2039.07.13	S	MK	683234MM7	BD	'99-'01	$300,000	$223,858	
5.700	2039.12.02	S	NE	683234NL8	BD	'00-'06	$1,489,000	$1,489,000	
6.200	2040.04.18	S	DMTN44	683234RF7	MN	'02-'05	$100,000	$100,000	
0.699	2040.10.02	A	EMTN118		BD	2020	€50,000	€50,000	
4.650	2041.06.02	S	DMTN204	683234B98	MN	'10-'11	$11,650,000	$11,650,000	1
1.820	2041.06.28	A	EMTN112		NT	2016	€52,000	€52,000	
6.200	2041.12.02	S	DMTN10	683234PS1	MN	'01-'06	$340,000	$340,000	
0.700	2041.12.09	A	EMTN125		BD	2021	€75,000	€75,000	
6.000	2042.03.08	S	DMTN29	683234QM3	MN	2001	$41,000	$41,000	
6.000	2042.06.02	S	DMTN33	683234QT8	MN	'02-'04	$240,000	$240,000	
3.500	2043.06.02	S	DMTN214	68323AAY0	MN	'12-'13	$11,200,000	$11,200,000	1
5.750	2043.06.02	S	DMTN62	683234SM1	MN	'03-'06	$75,000	$75,000	
4.600	2044.06.02	S	DMTN169	683234YR3	MN	2006	$27,000	$27,000	
Z.R.	2045.01.10		JL	683234JL3	BD	1995	$35,531	$35,531	17
9.500	2045.03.01	S	JK	683234JK5	BD	1995	$150,000	$150,000	18
4.500	2045.06.02	S	DMTN153	683234XP8	MN	'05-'06	$175,000	$175,000	
3.450	2045.06.02	S	DMTN220	68323ACC6	MN	'13-'14	$16,050,000	$16,050,000	1
4.850	2046.06.02	S	DMTN166	683234YN2	MN	'06-'07	$154,700	$154,700	
2.900	2046.12.02	S	DMTN228	68323ACY8	BD	'15-'16	$14,700,000	$14,700,000	1
0.760	2046.12.03	A	EMTN124		BD	2021	€160,000	€160,000	
4.500	2047.06.02	S	DMTN176	683234ZA9	MN	'07-'08	$158,000	$158,000	
4.700	2048.06.02	S	DMTN184	683234ZY7	MN	'08-'09	$50,000	$50,000	
2.800	2048.06.02	S	DMTN231	68323ADZ4	BD	'16-'17	$12,700,000	$12,700,000	
2.900	2049.06.02	S	DMTN236	68333ZAA5	BD	'17-'19	$13,250,000	$13,250,000	
2.650	2050.12.02	S	DMTN242	68333ZAG2	BD	'19-'20	$14,100,000	$14,100,000	
1.900	2051.12.02	S	DMTN246	68333ZAL1	BD	'20-'21	$12,750,000	$12,750,000	
2.550	2052.12.02	S	DMTN252	68333ZAS6	BD	'21-'22	$8,250,000	$8,250,000	
3.750	2053.12.02	S	DMTN255	68333ZAV9	BD	'22-'23	$12,400,000	$12,400,000	
4.600	2054.06.02	S	DMTN185	683234A24	MN	'08-'11	$40,000	$40,000	
4.150	2054.12.02	S		68333ZBA4	NT	'23-'24	$10,500,000	$12,000,000	
3.250	2062.06.02	S	DMTN216	68323ABP8	MN	'12-'23	$525,000	$525,000	

Provinces

GUARANTEED DEBT
March 31, 2024

Cpn %	Maturity	Freq	Series	CUSIP	Type	Year	Issued Amount (000)	Outstanding Amount (000)	Ref. Note
ONTARIO ELECTRICITY FINANCIAL CORPORATION									
8.500	2025.05.26	S	HYD-GB9	683078GB9	BD	1995	$500,000	$500,000	
9.000	2025.05.26	S	HYD-GD5	683078GD5	BD	1995	$500,000	$500,000	
8.250	2026.06.22	S	HYD-GG8	683078GG8	BD	1996	$1,000,000	$1,000,000	
6.594	2027.07.18	S	HYD-GR4	683078GR4	BD	1998	$114,900	$12,070	19
10.800	2031.04.11		HYD-FP9		BD	1991	$750,000	$750,000	20
6.000	2031.10.17	S	HYD-GT0-1	683078GT0	MN	1998	$100,000	$100,000	

REFERENCES
1. All or some of the amount issued is on-lent to Ontario Electricity Financial Corporation.
2. Interest is compounded and payable at maturity or, if redeemable, upon redemption.
3. Green bonds.
4. An additional $200,000,000 of series KR bonds were issued on Sept. 29, 1998 upon exchange of a similar amount of series LF bonds.
5. The terms of these debentures require that a one-time interest payment of $31.1 million be made at maturity.
6. Issued on Apr. 27, 1998 upon exchange of equal aggregate amount of 7.5% bonds due 2007.
7. Issued on Feb. 4, 1998 upon exchange of equal aggregate amount of 6.05% bonds due Feb. 4, 2002.
8. Green bonds issued under the Province's Sustainable Bond Framework.
9. Was retractable on Mar. 8, 2012 at par.
10. Extendible to Sept. 8, 2033 with an interest rate of 5.8%.
11. An additional $162,610,000 of series DMTN61 bonds were issued on Mar. 8, 2009 upon exchange of a similar amount of series DMTN102 bonds.
12. Zero coupon bonds which require unequal payments consisting of principal and interest to be made at predetermined irregular intervals. During the fiscal year 2010-11, principal repaid was $0.7 million. By Jan. 10, 2035, the principal to be repaid on these bonds will be $230,000,000.
13. Issued upon extension of equal aggregate amount of 9.5% bonds due Jan. 12, 2007.
14. Issued on Oct. 16, 2006 an additional $100,000,000 principal amount upon exchange of an equal amount of 5.6% bonds, series DMTN168, due June 2, 2035.
15. Was retractable on Dec. 2, 2014 at par. Previously, interest rate was 4.0%
16. Real return bonds.
17. The terms of these debentures require unequal payments, consisting of both principal and interest, to be made at predetermined irregular intervals with the final payment on Jan. 10, 2045. The total principal and interest to be payable over the life of the debenture is $1,325,000,000.
18. Was retractable on Mar. 1, 2010 at par.
19. Issued upon exchange of an equal amount of 5.682% bonds due July 18, 2003.
20. The annual coupons were stripped and the principal amount was restructured as a discount note which will mature at par.

Prince Edward Island

Premier: Dennis King (Progressive Conservative)
Capital City: Charlottetown
Area: 5,660 sq. kilometres

Visit this Web site:
   Province of Prince Edward Island: www.gov.pe.ca

DBRS Bond Rating at June 30, 2023 ... A

	2023	2022
Employed	91,900	84,300
Unemployment rate (%)	8.1	5.7
Average weekly earnings (Dec.)	$1,022.91	$985.86
Building permits	$534,531,000	$582,520,000
Retail sales	$3,564,352,000	$3,238,983,000
Population (est. July 1)	173,787	170,688
December consumer price index (2002=100)	163	158.8
Sales tax (HST)	15%	15%

DIRECT DEBT
March 31, 2024

Cpn %	Maturity	Freq	Series	CUSIP	Type	Year	Issued Amount (000)	Outstanding Amount (000)	Ref. Note
	**PROVINCE OF PRINCE EDWARD ISLAND**
2.350	2025.08.25	S		741666DA6	DB	2015	$125,000	$125,000	
6.100	2027.07.29	S		741666CN9	DB	2002	$100,000	$100,000	
1.200	2028.02.11	S		741666DC2	DB	2021	$125,000	$125,000	
6.800	2030.02.21	S		741666CL3	DB	2000	$80,000	$80,000	
1.850	2031.07.27	S		741666DD0	DB	'21-'22	$200,000	$200,000	
6.250	2032.01.29	S		741666CM1	DB	2002	$100,000	$100,000	
3.750	2032.12.01	S		741666DE8	DB	2023	$200,000	$200,000	
5.600	2034.02.21	S		741666CP4	DB	2003	$100,000	$100,000	
4.050	2034.06.02	S		741666DF5	DB	2024	$200,000	$200,000	
5.700	2035.06.15	S		741666CQ2	DB	2004	$100,000	$100,000	
5.300	2036.05.19	S		741666CR0	DB	2005	$100,000	$100,000	
4.650	2037.11.19	S		741666CS8	DB	'05-'10	$200,000	$200,000	
4.600	2041.05.19	S		741666CW9	DB	2011	$200,000	$200,000	
3.650	2042.06.27	S		741666CX7	DB	2012	$200,000	$200,000	
2.650	2051.12.01	S		741666DB4	DB	'19-'20	$225,000	$225,000	
3.600	2053.01.17	S		741666CY5	BD	'13-'14	$325,000	$325,000	
3.850	2054.07.17	S		741666CZ2	DB	2014	$125,000	$125,000	

GUARANTEED DEBT
March 31, 2024

Cpn %	Maturity	Freq	Series	CUSIP	Type	Year	Issued Amount (000)	Outstanding Amount (000)	Ref. Note
	**ISLAND WASTE MANAGEMENT CORPORATION**
6.400	2027.12.31	Q		464580AA7	NT	2002	$30,130	$7,939	

Québec

Premier: Francois Legault (Coalition Avenir Québec)
Capital City: Québec City
Area: 1,542,056 sq. kilometres

Visit these Web sites:
    Province of Québec: www.gouv.qc.ca
    Hydro-Québec: www.hydroquebec.com

DBRS Bond Rating at June 12, 2023 ... AA low

	2023	2022
Employed	4,531,900	4,464,200
Unemployment rate (%)	4.7	4.1
Average weekly earnings (Dec.)	$1,167.1	$1,129.54
Building permits	$25,182,247,000	$27,195,628,000
Retail sales	$177,698,376,000	$164,820,132,000
Population (est. July 1)	8,874,683	8,695,659
December consumer price index (2002=100)	155	149
Sales tax (GST)	5%	5%
(PST)	10%	10%

FP Bonds — Government 2024

DIRECT DEBT
March 31, 2024

Cpn %	Maturity	Freq	Series	CUSIP	Type	Year	Issued Amount (000)	Outstanding Amount (000)	Ref. Note
PROVINCE OF QUÉBEC									
2.500	2024.04.09	S	QW	748149AQ4	NT	2019	US$1,000,000	US$1,000,000	
3.750	2024.09.01	S	B113	74814ZES8	MN	'13-'14	$6,000,000	$6,000,000	
F.R.	2024.10.13	Q	B123	74814ZFC2	MN	2017	$1,500,000	$1,500,000	
2.875	2024.10.16	S	QO	748149AH4	BD	2014	US$1,600,000	US$1,600,000	
0.750	2024.11.21	A	E196		MN	2014	SFr375,000	SFr375,000	
0.750	2024.12.13	A	E208		MN	2019	£250,000	£250,000	
0.875	2025.01.15	A	E197		BD	2015	€1,750,000	€1,750,000	
1.500	2025.02.11	S	QX	748148RZ8	NT	2020	US$2,500,000	US$2,500,000	
4.200	2025.03.10	S	D006		MN	'14-'17	A$805,000	A$805,000	
0.200	2025.04.07	A	E210		BD	2020	€1,600,000	€1,600,000	
5.350	2025.06.01	S	B076	74814ZDE0	MN	'04-'07	$652,000	$652,000	
2.600	2025.07.06	S	QU	748148RX3	BD	2018	$500,000	$500,000	1
0.600	2025.07.23	S	RA	748148SC8	NT	2020	US$3,250,000	US$3,250,000	
2.750	2025.09.01	S	B116	74814ZEV1	MN	'15-'20	$7,200,000	$7,200,000	
1.125	2025.10.28	A	E198		MN	2015	€1,100,000	€1,100,000	
6.350	2026.01.30	S	49	74815HBZ4	MN	1996	US$150,000	US$149,875	2
7.140	2026.02.27	S	51	74815HCB6	MN	1996	US$100,000	US$99,770	3
7.485	2026.03.02	S		74815HCA8	MN	1996	US$150,000	US$150,000	
6.290	2026.03.06	S	52	74815HCC4	MN	1996	US$100,000	US$99,850	
7.035	2026.03.10	S	53	74815HCD2	MN	1996	US$50,000	US$50,000	4
8.500	2026.04.01	S	B033	74814ZBH5	MN	1996	$100,000	$100,000	
8.500	2026.04.01	S	B049	74814ZCA9	MN	1999	$90,000	$90,000	
7.500	2026.04.01	S	B067	74814ZDS9	MN	2002	$170,000	$165,850	5
5.500	2026.04.01	S	B070	74814ZCX9	MN	2003	$75,000	$74,332	
6.400	2026.04.01	S	B071	74814ZCY7	MN	2003	$90,000	$90,000	6
8.500	2026.04.01	S	OC	748148PZ0	BD	'96-'00	$2,176,100	$2,176,100	
7.380	2026.04.09	S	54	74815HCE0	MN	1996	US$100,000	US$100,000	
7.500	2026.04.15	S	55	74815HCF7	MN	1996	US$50,000	US$50,000	
7.500	2026.04.15	S	56	74815HCG5	MN	1996	US$50,000	US$50,000	7
2.500	2026.04.20	S	QP	748149AJ0	NT	2016	US$2,000,000	US$2,000,000	
3.700	2026.05.20	S	D007		MN	'15-'16	A$560,000	A$560,000	
7.295	2026.07.22	S	58	74815HCJ9	MN	1996	US$100,000	US$99,835	8
2.500	2026.09.01	S	B118	74814ZEX7	MN	2016	$6,000,000	$6,000,000	
2.250	2026.09.15	A	E215		MN	2022	£750,000	£750,000	
8.625	2026.12.01	S	KL	748148KA0	BD	1986	US$300,000	US$300,000	
4.500	2026.12.01	S	OP	748148QG1	BD	'98-'08	$859,920	$859,920	9
1.850	2027.02.13	S	QY	748148SA2	NT	2020	$500,000	$500,000	1
2.750	2027.04.12	S	QS	748149AN1	NT	2017	US$1,250,000	US$1,250,000	
0.875	2027.05.04	A	E200		MN	2017	€2,250,000	€2,250,000	
2.750	2027.09.01	S	B122	74814ZFB4	MN	'17-'18	$6,000,000	$6,000,000	
1.797	2028.01.01	Q	B092	74814ZDV2	MN	2008	$538,006	$122,467	
1.305	2028.03.21	S	E192		MN	2013	Jp¥5,000,000	Jp¥5,000,000	
6.100	2028.04.01	S		74814ZCD3	MN	1999	$5,000	$5,000	
3.625	2028.04.13	S	RC	748148SD6	NT	2023	US$3,500,000	US$3,500,000	
0.875	2028.07.05	A	E203		MN	2018	€1,000,000	€1,000,000	
2.750	2028.09.01	S	B124	74814ZFD0	MN	'18-'19	$6,000,000	$6,000,000	

FP Bonds — Government 2024

Cpn %	Maturity	Freq	Series	CUSIP	Type	Year	Issued Amount (000)	Outstanding Amount (000)	Ref. Note
3.250	2028.10.18	S	D008		MN	2018	A$160,000	A$160,000	
2.730	2029.04.03	S	E187		MN	2009	Jp¥13,000,000	Jp¥13,000,000	
2.854	2029.04.10	S	E206		MN	2019	NZ$66,000	NZ$66,000	
1.169	2029.04.11	A	E207		MN	2019	SKr1,700,000	SKr1,700,000	
2.900	2029.04.27	S	E189		MN	2009	Jp¥3,000,000	Jp¥3,000,000	
2.300	2029.09.01	S	B126	74814ZFF5	MN	'19-'20	$6,500,000	$6,500,000	
7.500	2029.09.15	S	PD	748148QR7	BD	1999	US$1,500,000	US$1,500,000	
6.000	2029.10.01	S	OS	748148QJ5	BD	'98-'02	$2,737,300	$2,737,300	
Z.R.	2029.10.15	A	E209		MN	2019	€1,000,000	€1,000,000	
2.600	2029.10.18	S	D009		MN	2019	A$100,000	A$100,000	
4.140	2030.03.12	A	QH		BD	2010	€75,000	€75,000	
4.020	2030.04.29	A	QI		BD	2010	€35,000	€35,000	
1.350	2030.05.28	S	QZ	748148SB0	NT	2020	US$1,500,000	US$1,500,000	
1.900	2030.09.01	S	B127	74814ZFG3	MN	2020	$10,800,000	$10,800,000	
Z.R.	2030.10.29	A	E211		NT	2020	€2,250,000	€2,250,000	
1.900	2031.04.21	S	RB	748149AR2	NT	2021	US$1,000,000	US$1,000,000	
0.250	2031.05.05	A	E212		MN	2021	€2,500,000	€2,500,000	
2.100	2031.05.27	S	B130	74814ZFM0	NT	2021	$500,000	$500,000	1
0.030	2031.06.18	A	E213		NT	2021	SFr250,000	SFr250,000	
1.500	2031.09.01	S	B128	74814ZFH1	BD	'21-'22	$9,000,000	$9,000,000	
4.250	2031.12.01	S	PM	748148QZ9	BD	'01-'08	$947,880	$947,880	9
3.441	2031.12.01	S	PS	748148RF2	BD	2002	$97,000	$14,157	9
3.500	2031.12.15	A	QL		MN	2011	€27,000	€27,000	
0.500	2032.01.25	A	E214		BD	2022	€2,250,000	€2,250,000	
3.650	2032.05.20	S	B132	74814ZFP3	BD	2022	$1,000,000	$1,000,000	1
6.250	2032.06.01	S	PH	748148QT3	BD	'00-'03	$4,200,200	$4,200,200	
3.250	2032.09.01	S	B131	74814ZFN8	MN	'22-'23	$8,400,000	$8,400,000	
3.900	2032.11.22	S	B134	74814ZFR9	MN	'22-'23	$1,400,000	$1,400,000	1
3.000	2033.01.24	A	E216		NT	2023	€2,250,000	€2,250,000	
3.650	2033.04.06	S	D010		MN	2022	A$60,000	A$60,000	
2.040	2033.05.09	A	E217		NT	2023	SFr390,000	SFr390,000	
3.600	2033.09.01	S	B135	74814ZFS7	MN	'23-'24	$10,950,000	$12,300,000	
4.500	2033.09.08	S	RD	748148SE4	NT	2023	US$1,500,000	US$1,500,000	
3.125	2034.03.27	A			MN	2024	€2,250,000	€2,250,000	
6.500	2035.04.01	S		74814ZBP7	MN	1997	$300,000	$300,000	
Z.R.	2035.04.01			74814ZCB7	MN	1999	$456,000	$456,000	
Z.R.	2035.04.01		B009	74814ZAH6	MN	1995	$150,000	$150,000	10
V.R.	2035.04.01		B018	74814ZAS2	MN	1995	$150,000	$150,000	10
V.R.	2035.04.01		B019	74814ZAT0	MN	1995	$100,000	$100,000	10
5.400	2035.11.17	S	A063	74815HCP5	MN	2005	US$75,000	US$75,000	
7.970	2036.07.22	S	57	748148QH9	MN	1996	US$160,000	US$160,000	11
3.250	2036.12.01	S	B093	74814ZDW0	BD	'08-'10	$724,205	$724,205	9
5.750	2036.12.01	S	PX	748148RL9	BD	'03-'06	$4,082,900	$4,082,900	
5.000	2038.12.01	S	B082	74814ZDK6	MN	'06-'09	$5,000,000	$5,000,000	
Z.R.	2039.10.01			74814ZCC5	MN	1999	$525,000	$525,000	
V.R.	2040.04.01		B057	74814ZCJ0	MN	'00-'01	$463,000	$463,000	10
5.000	2041.12.01	S	B102	74814ZEF6	MN	'09-'15	$9,200,000	$9,200,000	
5.600	2043.07.08	S	B069	74814ZCW1	MN	2003	$80,000	$80,000	
4.250	2043.12.01	S	B106	74814ZEK5	MN	'11-'17	$7,500,000	$7,500,000	
3.500	2045.12.01	S	B112	74814ZER0	MN	'13-'15	$10,000,000	$10,000,000	
3.500	2048.12.01	S	B117	74814ZEW9	MN	'15-'20	$11,650,000	$11,650,000	

Provinces

Cpn %	Maturity	Freq	Series	CUSIP	Type	Year	Issued Amount (000)	Outstanding Amount (000)	Ref. Note
5.100	2049.09.21	S	B094	74814ZDX8	MN	'08-'09	$13,440	$13,440	
5.000	2051.09.21	S	B085	74814ZDN0	MN	2006	$420,000	$420,000	
3.100	2051.12.01	S	B125	74814ZFE8	MN	'19-'21	$14,000,000	$14,000,000	
5.100	2053.09.21	S	B095	74814ZDY6	MN	'08-'09	$37,192	$37,192	
2.850	2053.12.01	S	B129	74814ZFL2	MN	'21-'22	$11,500,000	$11,500,000	
4.400	2055.12.01	S	B133	74814ZFQ1	MN	'22-'24	$10,250,000	$12,650,000	
Z.R.	2056.12.01		B081	74814ZDJ9	MN	2006	$1,500,000	$1,500,000	
5.100	2057.09.21	S	B096	74814ZDZ3	MN	2008	$9,857	$9,857	
5.100	2058.09.21	S	B097	74814ZEA7	MN	'08-'09	$38,326	$38,326	
5.100	2059.09.21	S	B098	74814ZEB5	MN	2008	$6,294	$6,294	
5.000	2061.09.21	S	B099	74814ZEC3	MN	2009	$25,000	$25,000	
6.700	2062.09.21	S	B086	74814ZDP5	MN	2006	$150,000	$150,000	
Z.R.	2065.06.01		B100	74814ZED1	MN	2009	$385,000	$385,000	
Z.R.	2065.06.01		B108	74814ZEM1	MN	2012	$335,000	$335,000	
6.350	2065.09.21	S	B084	74814ZDM2	MN	'06-'08	$940,000	$940,000	
Z.R.	2075.06.01		B109	74814ZEN9	MN	2012	$100,000	$100,000	
Z.R.	2076.12.01		B090	74814ZDT7	MN	2007	$500,000	$500,000	

GUARANTEED DEBT
March 31, 2024

Cpn %	Maturity	Freq	Series	CUSIP	Type	Year	Issued Amount (000)	Outstanding Amount (000)	Ref. Note
FINANCEMENT QUÉBEC									
5.250	2034.06.01	S	R	31739ZAG0	MN	'06-'10	$1,522,350	$1,522,350	
HYDRO-QUÉBEC									
F.R.	Perpetual	S	GL		BD	1986	US$400,000	US$71,630	12
F.R.	Perpetual	S	JT		BD	2023	US$128,440	US$128,440	13
8.050	2024.07.07	S	I0	448814EJ8	BD	'94-'95	US$1,000,000	US$999,950	
7.500	2024.11.07	S	0005	44889ZDZ6	MN	1996	$25,000	$25,000	
7.910	2024.11.18	S	B-124	44881HET7	MN	1994	US$25,000	US$25,000	
7.400	2025.03.28	S	B-125	44881HEU4	MN	1995	US$55,000	US$55,000	
6.270	2026.01.03	S	B-127	44881HEW0	MN	1996	US$50,000	US$50,000	
8.875	2026.03.01	S	GF	448814CP6	BD	1986	US$250,000	US$250,000	
8.250	2026.04.15	S	GH	448814CS0	BD	1986	US$250,000	US$250,000	
8.250	2027.01.15	S	GQ	448814CT8	BD	1987	US$250,000	US$250,000	
2.461	2027.03.02	S	0071	44889ZET9	MN	2017	$15,000	$15,000	
Z.R.	2027.04.15		0061	44889ZEH5	MN	'09-'11	$65,450	$65,450	
9.500	2027.04.30	S	B-63	44881HCK8	MN	1992	US$20,000	US$20,000	
6.625	2028.07.13	S	B-130	44881HEZ3	MN	1998	US$50,000	US$50,000	
2.000	2028.09.01	S	0082	44889ZFE1	MN	2022	$2,400,000	$2,400,000	
6.500	2029.01.16	S	0017	44889ZCK0	MN	1999	$75,000	$75,000	
Z.R.	2029.04.29		0081	44889ZFD3	MN	2021	$36,036	$36,036	
8.625	2029.06.15	S	HE	448814DB6	BD	1989	US$250,000	US$250,000	
3.400	2029.09.01	S	0086	44889ZFJ0	MN	'23-'24	$2,400,000	$2,400,000	
8.500	2029.12.01	S	HH	448814DC4	BD	1989	US$500,000	US$500,000	
9.375	2030.04.15	S	HK	448814DF7	BD	1990	US$500,000	US$500,000	
1.322	2030.06.30	S	0078	44889ZFA9	MN	2020	$35,169	$35,169	
9.500	2030.11.15	S	HQ	448814DL4	BD	1990	US$500,000	US$500,000	

FP Bonds — Government 2024

Cpn %	Maturity	Freq	Series	CUSIP	Type	Year	Issued Amount (000)	Outstanding Amount (000)	Ref. Note
11.000	2031.02.26	S	IH	448814EG4	BD	1993	$190,000	$190,000	
2.048	2031.03.02	S	0080	44889ZFC5	MN	2021	$10,000	$10,000	
Z.R.	2031.04.18		0085	44889ZFH4	MN	2022	$38,355	$38,355	
6.000	2031.08.15	S	0038	44889ZDG8	MN	2001	$30,000	$4,325	
6.000	2031.08.15	S	JG	448814GY3	BD	1999	$825,675	$825,675	14
2.729	2032.03.02	S	0083	44889ZFF8	MN	2022	$10,000	$10,000	
6.500	2035.01.16	S	0009	44889ZBF2	MN	'98-'00	$686,500	$686,500	
6.400	2035.01.16	S	0011	44889ZBH8	MN	1998	$50,000	$50,000	15
3.530	2035.01.16	S	0016	44889ZCJ3	MN	1998	$170,000	$170,000	15
6.500	2035.02.15	S	0019	44889ZCM6	MN	'99-'04	$3,794,000	$3,794,000	
Z.R.	2035.07.16		0012	44889ZBJ4	MN	1998	$150,000	$150,000	15
Z.R.	2035.07.16		0014		MN	1998	$73,500	$73,500	15
Z.R.	2039.04.15		0088	44889ZFL5	MN	2023	$20,000	$53,135	
6.000	2040.02.15	S	0020	44889ZCN4	MN	'99-'06	$3,770,500	$3,770,500	
5.000	2045.02.15	S	JM	448814HZ9	BD	'06-'08	$5,000,000	$5,000,000	
6.000	2050.02.15	S	0032	44889ZDA1	MN	2000	$50,000	$50,000	
5.000	2050.02.15	S	JN	448814JA2	BD	'09-'13	$7,000,000	$7,000,000	
4.000	2055.02.15	S	JQ	4488148V8	BD	'14-'20	$7,000,000	$7,000,000	
Z.R.	2060.02.15		0033	44889ZDB9	MN	'00-'01	$200,000	$200,000	15
Z.R.	2060.02.15		0037	44889ZDF0	MN	2001	$10,000	$10,000	15
Z.R.	2060.02.15		0039	44889ZDH6	MN	2001	$121,000	$121,000	
Z.R.	2060.02.15		0040	44889ZDJ2	MN	2001	$30,000	$30,000	15,16
2.100	2060.02.15	S	JR	448814JC8	DB	'20-'22	$6,500,000	$6,500,000	
4.000	2063.02.15	S	JS	448814JD6	DB	'22-'24	$5,000,000	$6,500,000	

CALLABLE BONDS
March 31, 2024

Coupon Rate %	Maturity Date	Next Call Date	Next Call Price	Call Flag
HYDRO-QUÉBEC				
F.R.	Perpetual	2024.09.09	US$100.00	P
F.R.	Perpetual	2024.03.31	US$100.00	P

REFERENCES
1. Green bonds.
2. Was retractable on Jan. 30, 2011, 2016 and 2021.
3. Was retractable on Feb. 27, 2016.
4. Was retractable on Mar. 10, 2008. Previously, interest rate was 6.185%.
5. Extendible to Apr. 1, 2026 with an interest rate of 7.5%.
6. Extendible to Apr. 1, 2026 with an interest rate of 6.4%.
7. Was retractable on Apr. 15, 2021.
8. Was retractable on July 22, 2006 and thereafter on interest payment dates.
9. Real return bonds. The bonds pay semiannual interest plus an adjustment based on the Canadian Consumer Price Index.
10. Terms of the notes include irregular blended payments of interest and principal.
11. Was retractable on July 22, 2016.
12. Interest rate is Synthetic LIBOR plus 0.0625%.
13. Interest rate is SOFR plus 0.49076%.
14. Outstanding amount includes $25,675,000 issued upon exchange of medium term notes with like terms.
15. Discount bonds.

16. Variable rate payable annually beginning Feb. 15, 2050.

Saskatchewan

Premier: Scott Moe (Saskatchewan Party)
Capital City: Regina
Area: 651,936 sq. kilometres

Visit this Web site:
Province of Saskatchewan: www.saskatchewan.ca

DBRS Bond Rating at July 18, 2023 ... AA low

	2023	2022
Employed	607,000	584,500
Unemployment rate (%)	5	4.4
Average weekly earnings (Dec.)	$1,170.89	$1,147.21
Building permits	$2,364,160,000	$2,122,834,000
Retail sales	$25,217,690,000	$24,522,816,000
Population (est. July 1)	1,209,107	1,194,803
December consumer price index (2002=100)	159.9	155.7

DIRECT DEBT
March 31, 2024

Cpn %	Maturity	Freq	Series	CUSIP	Type	Year	Issued Amount (000)	Outstanding Amount (000)	Ref. Note
PROVINCE OF SASKATCHEWAN									
3.200	2024.06.03	S		803854JW9	DB	'14-'20	$1,250,000	$1,250,000	
8.750	2025.05.30	S		803854FP8	DB	1995	$175,000	$175,000	
0.800	2025.09.02	S		803854KM9	DB	2020	$1,200,000	$1,200,000	
2.550	2026.06.02	S		803854KB3	DB	'16-'21	$1,575,000	$1,575,000	
2.650	2027.06.02	S		803854KE7	DB	2017	$1,000,000	$1,000,000	
3.250	2027.06.08	S		803854KQ0	BD	2022	US$1,000,000	US$1,000,000	
3.050	2028.12.02	S		803854KF4	DB	'18-'19	$1,300,000	$1,300,000	
5.600	2029.03.05	S		803854GZ5	MN	1999	$60,000	$60,000	
5.750	2029.03.05	S	SB	803854GY8	DB	'98-'00	$350,000	$350,000	
6.350	2030.01.25	S		803854JN9	MN	'00-'07	$200,000	$169,995	
6.250	2030.01.25	S		803854HF8	MN	2000	$25,000	$25,000	
2.200	2030.06.02	S	XC	803854KJ6	DB	'19-'21	$1,400,000	$1,400,000	
2.150	2031.06.02	S		803854KP2	DB	'21-'22	$1,600,000	$1,600,000	
6.400	2031.09.05	S	XB	803854HN1	DB	'01-'03	$550,000	$550,000	
6.300	2032.02.13	S		803854JR0	MN	2002	$30,000	$29,954	
0.525	2032.03.01	A			NT	2022	SFr100,000	SFr100,000	
3.900	2033.06.02	S		803854KU1	DB	'23-'24	$1,300,000	$1,700,000	
5.800	2033.09.05	S		803854JA7	DB	'03-'04	$450,000	$450,000	
5.800	2033.09.05	S		803854JB5	DB	'03-'04	$104,500	$104,500	1
5.600	2035.09.05	S	DC	803854JH2	DB	2004	$400,000	$400,000	
5.000	2037.03.05	S	EC	803854JJ8	DB	'05-'06	$425,000	$425,000	
4.750	2040.06.01	S		803854JL3	DB	'06-'10	$1,050,000	$1,050,000	
3.400	2042.02.03	S		803854JT6	DB	'12-'13	$800,000	$800,000	
5.700	2042.09.05	S		803854HY7	MN	2002	$50,000	$50,000	
3.900	2045.06.02	S	MC	803854JU3	DB	'13-'15	$1,450,000	$1,450,000	
2.750	2046.12.02	S		803854KA5	DB	'15-'16	$2,200,000	$2,200,000	
3.300	2048.06.02	S		803854KC1	DB	'16-'18	$2,125,000	$2,125,000	
3.100	2050.06.02	S		803854KH0	DB	'18-'20	$2,500,000	$2,500,000	
2.800	2052.12.02	S		803854KN7	DB	'21-'22	$1,600,000	$1,600,000	
3.750	2054.03.05	S		803854JX7	DB	'14-'17	$725,000	$725,000	
4.200	2054.12.02	S		803854KV9	DB	'23-'24	$1,000,000	$1,000,000	
2.950	2058.06.02	S		803854KG2	MN	'18-'23	$750,000	$750,000	
2.350	2060.06.02	S		803854KL1	MN	'20-'21	$310,000	$310,000	
3.800	2062.06.02	S		803854KT4	MN	2023	$300,000	$300,000	

REFERENCES
1. Extendible to Sept. 5, 2033 with an interest rate of 5.8%.

Eurobonds

Debts offered in the European market, listed alphabetically by government issuer.

EURO BONDS
March 31, 2024

Cpn %	Maturity	Freq	Series	Year	Issued Amount (000)	Outstanding Amount (000)
CPPIB CAPITAL INC.						
0.375	2024.06.20	A		2017	€2,000,000	€2,000,000
0.500	2024.09.16	S	34	2021	US$1,000,000	US$1,000,000
4.125	2024.10.21	S	52	2022	US$1,750,000	US$1,750,000
0.875	2024.12.17	A	17	2020	£500,000	£500,000
F.R.	2025.04.04	Q	47	2022	US$1,500,000	US$1,500,000
6.000	2025.06.07	A	58	2023	£1,000,000	£1,000,000
4.375	2026.03.02	A	56	2023	£750,000	£750,000
F.R.	2026.03.11	Q	40	2021	US$750,000	US$750,000
F.R.	2026.06.15	Q	37	2021	£750,000	£750,000
0.250	2027.04.06	A	19	2020	€1,000,000	€1,000,000
4.500	2027.07.22	A	63	2024	£600,000	£600,000
2.750	2027.11.02	S	4	2017	US$1,000,000	US$1,000,000
4.250	2028.07.20	S	59	2023	US$1,500,000	US$1,500,000
0.875	2029.02.06	A	12	2019	€1,000,000	€1,000,000
2.000	2029.11.01	S	15	2019	US$1,000,000	US$1,000,000
1.125	2029.12.14	A	23	2020	£750,000	£750,000
0.050	2031.02.24	A	31	2021	€1,000,000	€1,000,000
1.500	2033.03.04	A	6	2018	€1,000,000	€1,000,000
0.750	2037.02.02	A	46	2022	€1,000,000	€1,000,000
0.250	2041.01.18	A	28	2021	€1,000,000	€1,000,000
2.414	2041.02.25	S		2021	A$150,000	A$150,000
2.790	2041.03.12	S	33	2021	A$120,000	A$120,000
0.750	2049.07.15	A	13	2019	€1,000,000	€1,000,000
2.580	2051.02.23	S	30	2021	A$160,000	A$160,000
1.625	2071.10.22	A	43	2021	£900,000	£900,000
PROVINCE OF ALBERTA						
0.500	2025.04.16	A		2020	€1,100,000	€1,100,000
0.625	2025.04.18	A		2018	€1,500,000	€1,500,000
0.625	2026.01.16	A		2019	€1,250,000	€1,250,000
2.050	2026.08.17	S	PAGM06	2016	US$1,000,000	US$1,000,000
0.250	2028.04.20	A		2020	SFr260,000	SFr260,000
0.375	2029.02.07	A		2019	SFr325,000	SFr325,000
1.403	2029.02.20	A		2019	SKr2,500,000	SKr2,500,000
1.782	2040.12.03	A		'15-'16	€202,000	€202,000
3.225	2041.09.16	S		2021	NZ$128,000	NZ$128,000
1.150	2043.12.01	A		'16-'17	€435,000	€435,000
0.925	2045.05.08	A		2020	€70,000	€70,000
1.413	2050.03.31	A		2020	€30,000	€30,000
1.500	2050.04.07	A		2020	€90,000	€90,000
PROVINCE OF BRITISH COLUMBIA						
0.875	2025.10.08	A	BCEURO-2	2015	€500,000	€500,000
2.500	2030.04.18	A	BCSFR-7	2010	SFr100,000	SFr100,000
0.700	2032.07.20	A	BCEURO-5	2016	€250,000	€250,000
3.000	2034.07.24	A	BCEURO-17	2024	€1,250,000	€1,250,000

Cpn %	Maturity	Freq	Series	Year	Issued Amount (000)	Outstanding Amount (000)
1.337	2037.01.27	A	BCEURO-6	2017	€150,000	€150,000
3.210	2038.11.08	A	BCEURO-1	2011	€40,000	€40,000
3.741	2039.04.01	A	BCEURO-16	2023	€100,000	€100,000
3.508	2039.06.07	A	EURO-14	2023	€86,000	€86,000
2.060	2039.06.09	A	BCEURO-13	2022	€100,000	€100,000
1.678	2040.12.18	A	BCEURO-3	2015	€75,000	€75,000
0.590	2042.12.22	A	BCEURO-12	2021	€135,000	€135,000
1.250	2043.06.17	A	BCEURO-4	2016	€100,000	€100,000
1.227	2044.04.25	A	BCEURO-7	2019	€130,000	€130,000
1.000	2048.04.09	A	BCEURO-11	2020	€170,000	€170,000
0.478	2049.10.18	A	BCEURO-9	'19-'23	€709,000	€709,000
0.270	2050.03.30	A	BCEURO-10	2020	€150,000	€150,000
3.402	2053.06.05	A	BCEURO-15	2023	€80,000	€80,000

PROVINCE OF MANITOBA

Cpn %	Maturity	Freq	Series	Year	Issued Amount (000)	Outstanding Amount (000)
0.200	2026.04.20	A		2020	SFr100,000	SFr100,000
0.250	2029.03.15	A		2019	SFr250,000	SFr250,000
2.915	2029.04.10	S	C169	2019	NZ$39,500	NZ$39,500
1.252	2034.07.18	A		2019	SKr500,000	SKr500,000
0.600	2035.03.30	A		2020	€60,000	€60,000
1.390	2035.06.11	A	C142	2015	€32,000	€32,000
0.750	2037.02.02	A		2022	€70,000	€70,000
3.740	2037.02.16	A		2022	NZ$130,000	NZ$130,000
0.800	2039.03.15	A		2019	SFr150,000	SFr150,000
1.000	2039.06.25	A	C154	2016	€40,000	€40,000
0.700	2040.04.20	A		2020	SFr100,000	SFr100,000
1.770	2040.06.25	A	C143	'15-'16	€470,000	€470,000
1.740	2041.02.25	A	C147	2016	€85,000	€85,000
1.500	2041.06.25	A	C151	'16-'19	€285,000	€285,000
1.950	2041.06.25	A	H062	2016	€45,000	€45,000
0.700	2041.11.25	A		2021	€160,000	€160,000
0.800	2046.04.27	S	C149	2016	Jp¥5,000,000	Jp¥5,000,000
0.700	2046.08.30	S	C153	2016	Jp¥6,000,000	Jp¥6,000,000
0.700	2046.12.05	S	C156	2016	Jp¥5,000,000	Jp¥5,000,000
1.500	2049.06.25	A	C170	2019	€100,000	€100,000
1.250	2049.06.25	A	C176	2020	€75,000	€75,000
0.475	2049.11.02	A		2020	€100,000	€100,000

PROVINCE OF NEW BRUNSWICK

Cpn %	Maturity	Freq	Series	Year	Issued Amount (000)	Outstanding Amount (000)
0.250	2029.01.19	A	HV	'17-'18	SFr300,000	SFr300,000
0.200	2031.11.07	A	HU	2016	SFr400,000	SFr400,000
0.125	2032.12.06	A	IE	2019	SFr100,000	SFr100,000
0.250	2039.12.06	A	ID	2019	SFr125,000	SFr125,000

PROVINCE OF ONTARIO

Cpn %	Maturity	Freq	Series	Year	Issued Amount (000)	Outstanding Amount (000)
1.875	2024.05.21	A	EMTN110	2014	€1,750,000	€1,750,000
0.375	2024.06.14	A	EMTN114	2017	€1,500,000	€1,500,000
0.875	2025.01.21	A	EMTN111	2015	€1,250,000	€1,250,000
0.625	2025.04.17	A	EMTN116	2018	€1,500,000	€1,500,000
2.250	2026.05.26	A	EMTN126	2022	£500,000	£500,000
0.250	2026.12.15	A	EMTN121	2021	£1,750,000	£1,750,000
0.375	2027.04.08	A	EMTN117	2020	€1,000,000	€1,000,000

Cpn %	Maturity	Freq	Series	Year	Issued Amount (000)	Outstanding Amount (000)
0.250	2029.06.28	A	EMTN115	2017	SFr400,000	SFr400,000
0.010	2030.11.25	A	EMTN120	2020	€2,500,000	€2,500,000
0.250	2031.06.09	A	EMTN123	2021	€1,000,000	€1,000,000
0.050	2033.05.12	A	EMTN122	2021	SFr250,000	SFr250,000
3.100	2034.01.31	A	EMTN127	2024	€1,250,000	€1,250,000
9.400	2034.07.13	S	EMTN5	1994	$300,000	$300,000
0.699	2040.10.02	A	EMTN118	2020	€50,000	€50,000
1.820	2041.06.28	A	EMTN112	2016	€52,000	€52,000
0.700	2041.12.09	A	EMTN125	2021	€75,000	€75,000
0.760	2046.12.03	A	EMTN124	2021	€160,000	€160,000

PROVINCE OF QUÉBEC

Cpn %	Maturity	Freq	Series	Year	Issued Amount (000)	Outstanding Amount (000)
0.750	2024.11.21	A	E196	2014	SFr375,000	SFr375,000
0.750	2024.12.13	A	E208	2019	£250,000	£250,000
0.875	2025.01.15	A	E197	2015	€1,750,000	€1,750,000
0.200	2025.04.07	A	E210	2020	€1,600,000	€1,600,000
1.125	2025.10.28	A	E198	2015	€1,100,000	€1,100,000
2.250	2026.09.15	A	E215	2022	£750,000	£750,000
0.875	2027.05.04	A	E200	2017	€2,250,000	€2,250,000
1.305	2028.03.21	S	E192	2013	Jp¥5,000,000	Jp¥5,000,000
0.875	2028.07.05	A	E203	2018	€1,000,000	€1,000,000
2.730	2029.04.03	S	E187	2009	Jp¥13,000,000	Jp¥13,000,000
2.854	2029.04.10	S	E206	2019	NZ$66,000	NZ$66,000
1.169	2029.04.11	A	E207	2019	SKr1,700,000	SKr1,700,000
2.900	2029.04.27	S	E189	2009	Jp¥3,000,000	Jp¥3,000,000
Z.R.	2029.10.15	A	E209	2019	€1,000,000	€1,000,000
4.140	2030.03.12	A	QH	2010	€75,000	€75,000
4.020	2030.04.29	A	QI	2010	€35,000	€35,000
Z.R.	2030.10.29	A	E211	2020	€2,250,000	€2,250,000
0.250	2031.05.05	A	E212	2021	€2,500,000	€2,500,000
0.030	2031.06.18	A	E213	2021	SFr250,000	SFr250,000
3.500	2031.12.15	A	QL	2011	€27,000	€27,000
0.500	2032.01.25	A	E214	2022	€2,250,000	€2,250,000
3.000	2033.01.24	A	E216	2023	€2,250,000	€2,250,000
2.040	2033.05.09	A	E217	2023	SFr390,000	SFr390,000
3.125	2034.03.27	A		2024	€2,250,000	€2,250,000

HYDRO-QUÉBEC

Cpn %	Maturity	Freq	Series	Year	Issued Amount (000)	Outstanding Amount (000)
F.R.	Perpetual	S	GL	1986	US$400,000	US$71,630
F.R.	Perpetual	S	JT	2023	US$128,440	US$128,440

PROVINCE OF SASKATCHEWAN

Cpn %	Maturity	Freq	Series	Year	Issued Amount (000)	Outstanding Amount (000)
0.525	2032.03.01	A		2022	SFr100,000	SFr100,000

CANADA'S INFORMATION RESOURCE CENTRE (CIRC)

Access all these great resources online, all the time, at Canada's Information Resource Centre (CIRC)
http://circ.greyhouse.ca

Canada's Information Resource Centre (CIRC) integrates all of Grey House Canada's award-winning reference content into one easy-to-use online resource. With **over 100,000 Canadian organizations** and **over 140,600 contacts**, plus thousands of additional facts and figures, CIRC is the most comprehensive resource for specialized database content in Canada! Access all 20 databases, including the recently revised *Careers & Employment Canada*, with Canada Info Desk Complete - it's the total package!

KEY ADVANTAGES OF CIRC:

- Seamlessly cross-database search content from select databases
- Save search results for future reference
- Link directly to websites or email addresses
- Clear display of your results makes compiling and adding to your research easier than ever before

DESIGN YOUR OWN CUSTOM CONTACT LISTS!

CIRC gives you the option to define and extract your own lists in seconds. Find new business leads, do keyword searches, locate upcoming conference attendees; all the information you want is right at your fingertips.

Brand new Major Canadian Cities data!

CHOOSE BETWEEN KEYWORD AND ADVANCED SEARCH!

With CIRC, you can choose between Keyword and Advanced search to pinpoint information. Designed for both beginner and advanced researchers, you can conduct simple text searches as well as powerful Boolean searches.

PROFILES IN CIRC INCLUDE:

- Phone numbers, email addresses, fax numbers and full addresses for all branches of the organization
- Social media accounts, such as Twitter and Facebook
- Key contacts based on job titles
- Budgets, membership fees, staff sizes and more!

Search CIRC using common or unique fields, customized to your needs!

ONLY GREY HOUSE DIRECTORIES PROVIDE SPECIAL CONTENT YOU WON'T FIND ANYWHERE ELSE!

- **Associations Canada:** finances/funding sources, activities, publications, conferences, membership, awards, member profile
- **Canadian Parliamentary Guide:** private and political careers of elected members, complete list of constituencies and representatives
- **Financial Services:** type of ownership, number of employees, year founded, assets, revenue, ticker symbol
- **Libraries Canada:** staffing, special collections, services, year founded, national library symbol, regional system
- **Governments Canada:** municipal population
- **Canadian Who's Who:** birth city, publications, education (degrees, alma mater), career/occupation and employer
- **Major Canadian Cities:** demographics, ethnicity, immigration, language, education, housing, income, labour and transportation
- **Health Guide Canada:** chronic and mental illnesses, general resources, appendices and statistics
- **Cannabis Canada:** firm type, foreign activity, type of ownership, revenue sources
- **Canadian Environmental Resource Guide:** organization scope, budget, number of employees, activities, regulations, areas of environmental specialty
- **Careers & Employment Canada:** career associations, career employment websites, expanded employers, recruiters, awards and scholarships, and summer jobs
- **FP Directory of Directors:** names, directorships, educational and professional backgrounds and email addresses of top Canadian directors; list of major companies and complete company contact information
- **FPbonds:** bond information in PDF form and with sortable tables
- **FPsurvey:** detailed profiles of current publicly traded companies, as well as past corporate changes

The new CIRC provides easier searching and faster, more pinpointed results of all of our great resources in Canada, from Associations and Government to Major Companies to Zoos and everything in between. Whether you need fully detailed information on your contact or just an email address, you can customize your search query to meet your needs.

Contact us now for a **free trial** subscription or visit http://circ.greyhouse.ca

---

GREY HOUSE PUBLISHING CANADA For more information please contact Grey House Publishing Canada
Tel.: (866) 433-4739 or (416) 644-6479 Fax: (416) 644-1904 | info@greyhouse.ca | www.greyhouse.ca

CENTRE DE DOCUMENTATION DU CANADA (CDC)

Consultez en tout temps toutes ces excellentes ressources en ligne grâce au Centre de documentation du Canada (CDC) à
http://circ.greyhouse.ca

Le Centre de documentation du Canada (CDC) regroupe sous une seule ressource en ligne conviviale tout le contenu des ouvrages de référence primés de Grey House Canada. Répertoriant plus de **100 000 entreprises canadiennes, et plus de 140 600 personnes-ressources**, faits et chiffres, il s'agit de la ressource la plus complète en matière de bases de données spécialisées au Canada! Grâce à l'ajout de sept bases de données, le Canada Info Desk Complete est plus avantageux que jamais alors qu'il coûte 50 % que l'abonnement aux ouvrages individuels. Accédez aux 20 bases de données dès maintenant – le Canadian Info Desk Complete vous offre un ensemble complet!

PRINCIPAUX AVANTAGES DU CDC

- Recherche transversale efficace dans le contenu des bases de données
- Sauvegarde des résultats de recherche pour consultation future
- Lien direct aux sites Web et aux adresses électroniques
- Grâce à l'affichage lisible de vos résultats, il est dorénavant plus facile de compiler les résultats ou d'ajouter des critères à vos recherches

Nouvelles données sur les Principales villes canadiennes!

CONCEPTION PERSONNALISÉE DE VOS LISTES DE PERSONNES-RESSOURCES!

Le CDC vous permet de définir et d'extraire vos propres listes, et ce, en quelques secondes.
Découvrez des clients potentiels, effectuez des recherches par mot-clé, trouvez les participants à une conférence à venir : l'information dont vous avez besoin, au bout de vos doigts.

CHOISISSEZ ENTRE RECHERCHES MOT-CLÉ ET AVANCÉE!

Grâce au CDC, vous pouvez choisir entre une recherche Mot-clé ou Avancée pour localiser l'information avec précision. Vous avez la possibilité d'effectuer des recherches en texte simple ou booléennes puissantes – les recherches sont conçues à l'intention des chercheurs débutants et avancés.

LES PROFILS DU CDC COMPRENNENT :

- Numéros de téléphone, adresses électroniques, numéros de télécopieur et adresses complètes pour toutes les succursales d'un organisme
- Comptes de médias sociaux, comme Twitter et Facebook
- Personnes-ressources clés en fonction des appellations d'emploi
- Budgets, frais d'adhésion, tailles du personnel et plus!

Effectuez des recherches dans le CDC à l'aide de champs uniques ou communs, personnalisés selon vos besoins!

SEULS LES RÉPERTOIRES DE GREY HOUSE VOUS OFFRENT UN CONTENU PARTICULIER QUE VOUS NE TROUVEREZ NULLE PART AILLEURS!

- **Le répertoire des associations du Canada** : sources de financement, activités, publications, congrès, membres, prix, profil de membre
- **Guide parlementaire canadien** : carrières privées et politiques des membres élus, liste complète des comtés et des représentants
- **Services financiers** : type de propriétaire, nombre d'employés, année de la fondation, immobilisations, revenus, symbole au téléscripteur
- **Bibliothèques Canada** : personnel, collections particulières, services, année de la fondation, symbole de bibliothèque national, système régional
- **Gouvernements du Canada** : population municipale
- **Canadian Who's Who** : ville d'origine, publication, formation (diplômes et alma mater), carrière/emploi et employeur
- **Principales villes canadiennes** : données démographiques, ethnicité, immigration, langue, éducation, logement, revenu, main-d'œuvre et transport
- **Guide canadien de la santé** : maladies chroniques et mentales, ressources generales, annexes et statistiques
- **Cannabis au Canada** : type d'entreprise, activité à l'étranger, type de propriété, sources de revenus
- **Guide des ressources environnementales canadiennes** : périmètre organisationnel, budget, nombre d'employés, activités, réglementations, domaines de spécialité environnementale
- **Carrières et emplois Canada** : associations professionnelles, sites Web d'emplois, employeurs, recruteurs, bourses, et emplois d'été
- **Répertoire des administrateurs** : prénom, nom de famille, poste de cadre et d'administrateur, parcours scolaire et professionnel et adresse électronique des cadres supérieurs canadiens; liste des sociétés les plus importantes au Canada et l'information complète des compagnies
- **FPbonds** : information sur les obligations en format PDF, avec tableaux à trier
- **FPsurvey** : profils détaillés de sociétés cotées en bourse et changements organisationnels antérieurs

Le nouveau CDC facilite la recherche au sein de toutes nos ressources au Canada et procure plus rapidement des résultats plus poussés – des associations au gouvernement en passant par les principales entreprises et les zoos, sans oublier tout un éventail d'organisations! Que vous ayez besoin d'information très détaillée au sujet de votre personne-ressource ou d'une simple adresse électronique, vous pouvez personnaliser votre requête afin qu'elle réponde à vos besoins. Contactez-nous sans tarder pour obtenir un **essai gratuit** ou visitez http://circ.greyhouse.ca

---

GREY HOUSE PUBLISHING CANADA Pour obtenir plus d'information, veuillez contacter Grey House Publishing Canada
par tél. : 1 866 433-4739 ou 416 644-6479 par téléc. : 416 644-1904 | info@greyhouse.ca | www.greyhouse.ca

Canadian Almanac & Directory
The Definitive Resource for Facts & Figures About Canada

The *Canadian Almanac & Directory* has been Canada's most authoritative sourcebook for 177 years. Published annually since 1847, it continues to be widely used by publishers, business professionals, government offices, researchers, information specialists and anyone needing current, accessible information on every imaginable topic relevant to those who live and work in Canada.

A directory and a guide, the *Canadian Almanac & Directory* provides the most comprehensive picture of Canada, from physical attributes to economic and business summaries, leisure and recreation. It combines textual materials, charts, colour photographs and directory listings with detailed profiles, all verified and organized for easy retrieval. The *Canadian Almanac & Directory* is a wealth of general information, displaying national statistics on population, employment, CPI, imports and exports, as well as images of national awards, Canadian symbols, flags, emblems and Canadian parliamentary leaders.

For important contacts throughout Canada, for any number of business projects or for that once-in-a-while critical fact, the *Canadian Almanac & Directory* will help you find the leads you didn't even know existed—quickly and easily!

ALL THE INFORMATION YOU'LL EVER NEED, ORGANIZED INTO 17 DISTINCT CATEGORIES FOR EASY NAVIGATION!

Almanac—a fact-filled snapshot of Canada, including History, Geography, Economics and Vital Statistics.

Arts & Culture—includes 9 topics from Galleries to Zoos.

Associations—thousands of organizations arranged in over 120 different topics, from Accounting to Youth.

Broadcasting—Canada's major Broadcasting Companies, Provincial Radio and Television Stations, Cable Companies, and Specialty Broadcasters.

Business & Finance—Accounting, Banking, Insurance, Canada's Major Companies and Stock Exchanges.

Education—arranged by Province and includes Districts, Government Agencies, Specialized and Independent Schools, Universities and Technical facilities.

Government—spread over three sections, with a Quick Reference Guide, Federal and Provincial listings, County and Municipal Districts and coverage of Courts in Canada.

Health—Government agencies, hospitals, community health centres, retirement care and mental health facilities.

Law Firms—all Major Law Firms, followed by smaller firms organized by Province and listed alphabetically.

Libraries—Canada's main Library/Archive and Government Departments for Libraries, followed by Provincial listings and Regional Systems.

Publishing—Books, Magazines and Newspapers organized by Province, including frequency and circulation figures.

Religion—broad information about religious groups and associations from 37 different denominations.

Sports—Associations in 110 categories, with detailed League and Team listings.

Transportation—complete listings for all major modes.

Utilities—Associations, Government Agencies and Provincial Utility Companies.

PRINT OR ONLINE – QUICK AND EASY ACCESS TO ALL THE INFORMATION YOU NEED!

Available in hardcover print or electronically via the web, the *Canadian Almanac & Directory* provides instant access to the people you need and the facts you want every time.

Canadian Almanac & Directory print edition is verified and updated annually. Ongoing changes are added to the web version on a regular basis. The web version allows you to narrow your search by using index fields such as name or type of organization, subject, location, contact name or title and postal code.

Online subscribers have the option to instantly generate their own contact lists and export them into spreadsheets for further use—a great alternative to high cost list broker services.

GREY HOUSE PUBLISHING CANADA

For more information please contact Grey House Publishing Canada
Tel.: (866)-433-4739 or (416) 644-6479 Fax: (416) 644-1904 | info@greyhouse.ca | www.greyhouse.ca

Répertoire et almanach canadien
La ressource de référence au sujet des données et des faits relatifs au Canada

Le *Répertoire et almanach canadien* constitue le guide canadien le plus rigoureux depuis 177 ans. Publié annuellement depuis 1847, il est toujours grandement utilisé dans le monde des affaires, les bureaux gouvernementaux, par les spécialistes de l'information, les chercheurs, les éditeurs ou quiconque est à la recherche d'information actuelle et accessible sur tous les sujets imaginables à propos des gens qui vivent et travaillent au Canada.

À la fois répertoire et guide, le *Répertoire et almanach canadien* dresse le tableau le plus complet du Canada, des caractéristiques physiques jusqu'aux revues économique et commerciale, en passant par les loisirs et les activités récréatives. Il combine des documents textuels, des représentations graphiques, des photographies en couleurs et des listes de répertoires accompagnées de profils détaillés. Autant d'information pointue et organisée de manière à ce qu'elle soit facile à obtenir. Le *Répertoire et almanach canadien* foisonne de renseignements généraux. Il présente des statistiques nationales sur la population, l'emploi, l'IPC, l'importation et l'exportation ainsi que des images des prix nationaux, des symboles canadiens, des drapeaux, des emblèmes et des leaders parlementaires canadiens.

Si vous cherchez des personnes-ressources essentielles un peu partout au Canada, peu importe qu'il s'agisse de projets d'affaires ou d'une question factuelle anecdotique, le Répertoire et almanach canadien vous fournira les pistes dont vous ignoriez l'existence – rapidement et facilement!

TOUTE L'INFORMATION DONT VOUS AUREZ BESOIN, ORGANISÉE EN 17 CATÉGORIES DISTINCTES POUR UNE CONSULTATION FACILE!

Almanach—un aperçu informatif du Canada, notamment l'histoire, la géographie, l'économie et les statistiques essentielles.

Arts et culture—comprends 9 sujets, des galeries aux zoos.

Associations—des milliers d'organisations classées selon plus de 120 sujets différents, de l'actuariat au jeunesse.

Radiodiffusion—les principales sociétés de radiodiffusion au Canada, les stations radiophoniques et de télévision ainsi que les entreprises de câblodistribution et les diffuseurs thématiques.

Commerce et finance—comptabilité, services bancaires, assurances, principales entreprises et bourses canadiennes.

Éducation—organisé par province et comprend les arrondissements scolaires, les organismes gouvernementaux, les écoles spécialisées et indépendantes, les universités et les établissements techniques.

Gouvernement—s'étend sur trois sections et comprend un guide de référence, des listes fédérales et provinciales, les comtés et arrondissements municipaux ainsi que les cours canadiennes.

Santé—organismes gouvernementaux, hôpitaux, centres de santé communautaires, établissements de soins pour personnes retraitées et de soins de santé mentale.

Sociétés d'avocats—toutes les principales sociétés d'avocats, suivies des sociétés plus petites, classées par province et en ordre alphabétique.

Bibliothèques—la bibliothèque et les archives principales du Canada ainsi que les bibliothèques des ministères, suivis des listes provinciales et des systèmes régionaux.

Édition—livres, magazines et journaux classés par province, y compris leur fréquence et les données relatives à leur diffusion.

Religion—information générale au sujet des groupes religieux et des associations religieuses de 37 dénominations.

Sports—associations de 110 sports distincts; comprend des listes de ligues et d'équipes.

Transport—des listes complètes des principaux modes de transport.

Services publics—associations, organismes gouvernementaux et entreprises de services publics provinciales.

FORMAT PAPIER OU EN LIGNE – ACCÈS RAPIDE À TOUS LES RENSEIGNEMENTS DONT VOUS AVEZ BESOIN!

Offert sous couverture rigide ou en format électronique grâce au web, le *Répertoire et almanach canadien* offre invariablement un accès instantané aux représentants du gouvernement et aux faits qui font l'objet de vos recherches.

La version imprimée du Répertoire et almanach canadien est vérifiée et mise à jour annuellement. La version en ligne est mise à jour mensuellement. Cette version vous permet de circonscrire la recherche grâce aux champs de l'index comme le nom ou le type d'organisme, le sujet, l'emplacement, le nom ou le titre de la personne-ressource et le code postal.

Les abonnés au service en ligne peuvent générer instantanément leurs propres listes de contacts et les exporter en format feuille de calcul pour une utilisation approfondie – une solution de rechange géniale aux services dispendieux d'un commissionnaire en publipostage.

GREY HOUSE PUBLISHING CANADA

Pour obtenir plus d'information, veuillez contacter Grey House Publishing Canada
par tél. : 1 866 433-4739 ou 416 644-6479 par téléc. : 416 644-1904 | info@greyhouse.ca | www.greyhouse.ca

Major Canadian Cities
Compared & Ranked

New edition with 2021 census data!

Major Canadian Cities provides the user with numerous ways to rank and compare 50 major cities across Canada. All statistical information is at your fingertips; you can access details about the cities, each with a population of 100,000 or more. On Canada's Information Resource Centre (CIRC), you can instantly rank cities according to your preferences and make your own analytical tables with the data provided. There are hundreds of questions that these ranking tables will answer: Which cities have the youngest population? Where is the economic growth the strongest? Which cities have the best labour statistics?

A city profile for each location offers additional insights into the city to provide a sense of the location, its history, its recreational and cultural activities. Following the profile are rankings showing its uniqueness in the spectrum of cities across Canada: interesting notes about the city and how it ranks amongst the top 50 in different ways, such as most liveable, wealthiest and coldest! These reports are available only from Grey House Publishing Canada and only with your subscription to this exciting product!

AVAILABLE ONLINE!

Major Canadian Cities is available electronically via the Web, providing instant access to the facts you want about each city, as well as some interesting points showing how the city scores compared with others.

Use the online version to search statistics and create your own tables, or view pre-prepared tables in pdf form. This can help with research for academic work, infrastructure development or pure interest, with all the data you need in one, modifiable source.

MAJOR CANADIAN CITIES SHOWS YOU THESE STATISTICAL TABLES:

Demographics
- Population Growth
- Age Characteristics
- Male/Female Ratio
- Marital Status

Housing
- Household Type & Size
- Housing Age & Value

Labour
- Labour Force
- Occupation
- Industry
- Place of Work

Ethnicity, Immigration & Language
- Mother Tongue
- Knowledge of Official Languages
- Language Spoken at Home
- Minority Populations
- Education
- Education Attainment

Income
- Median Income
- Median Income After Taxes
- Median Income by Family Type
- Median Income After Taxes by Family Type

Transportation
- Mode of Transportation to Work

GREY HOUSE PUBLISHING CANADA For more information please contact Grey House Publishing Canada
Tel.: (866)-433-4739 or (416) 644-6479 Fax: (416) 644-1904 | info@greyhouse.ca | www.greyhouse.ca

Principales villes canadiennes
Comparaison et classement

Nouvelle édition avec les données du recensement de 2021 !

Principales villes canadiennes offre à l'utilisateur de nombreuses manières de classer et de comparer 50 villes principales du Canada. Toute l'information statistique se trouve au bout de vos doigts : vous pouvez obtenir des détails sur les villes, chacune comptant 100 000 habitants ou plus. Dans le Centre de documentation du Canada (CDC), vous pouvez classer instantanément les villes selon vos préférences et créer vos propres tableaux analytiques à l'aide des données fournies. Ces tableaux de classement répondent à des centaines de questions, notamment : quelles villes comptent la population la plus jeune? À quel endroit la croissance économique est-elle la plus forte? Quelles villes présentent les meilleures statistiques en matière de main-d'œuvre?

Un profil de ville offre des renseignements supplémentaires afin de vous donner une idée de son emplacement, de son histoire, de ses activités récréatives et culturelles. Suivent des classements qui démontrent l'unicité de la ville dans un spectre de villes qui se trouvent partout au Canada. Vous trouverez également des remarques intéressantes au sujet de la ville et de son classement parmi les 50 principales villes, par exemple selon celle où il fait le mieux vivre, où se trouvent les plus riches et où il fait le plus froid. Ces rapports sont disponibles uniquement auprès de Grey House Publishing Canada et dans le cadre de votre abonnement à ce produit emballant!

PRINCIPALES VILLES CANADIENNES COMPREND CES TABLEAUX STATISTIQUES :

Données démographiques
- Croissance de la population
- Caractéristiques relatives à l'âge
- Ratio homme/femme
- État matrimonial

Logement
- Type et taille du logement
- Âge et valeur du logement

Main-d'œuvre
- Population active
- Emploi
- Industrie
- Lieu de travail

Ethnicité, immigration et langue
- Langue maternelle
- Connaissance des langues officielles
- Langue parlée à la maison
- Populations minoritaires
- Formation
- Niveau scolaire

Revenu
- Revenu médian
- Revenu médian après impôts
- Revenu médian par type de famille
- Revenu médian après impôts par type de famille

Transport
- Moyen de transport vers le travail

OFFERT EN VERSION ÉLECTRONIQUE!

Principales villes canadiennes est offert en version électronique sur le Web. Vous accédez donc instantanément aux faits dont vous avez besoin pour chaque ville, de même que des éléments intéressants qui illustrent la comparaison entre les villes.

Servez-vous de la version en ligne pour effectuer des recherches parmi les statistiques et créer vos propres tableaux, ou consulter les tableaux déjà prêts en format PDF. Elle peut vous aider dans le cadre de recherches pour des travaux universitaires, pour le développement d'infrastructures ou consultez-la par simple curiosité – autant de données réunies en une source modifiable.

GREY HOUSE PUBLISHING CANADA

Pour obtenir plus d'information, veuillez contacter Grey House Publishing Canada
par tél. : 1 866 433-4739 ou 416 644-6479 par téléc. : 416 644-1904 | info@greyhouse.ca | www.greyhouse.ca

Canadian Who's Who

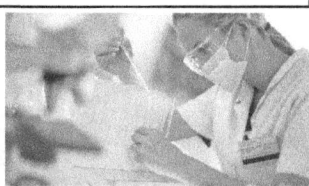

Canadian Who's Who is the only authoritative publication of its kind in Canada, offering access to the top 10 000 notable Canadians in all walks of life. Published annually to provide current and accurate information, the familiar bright-red volume is recognized as the standard reference source of contemporary Canadian biography.

Documenting the achievement of Canadians from a wide variety of occupations and professions, *Canadian Who's Who* records the diversity of culture in Canada. These biographies are organized alphabetically and provide detailed information on the accomplishments of notable Canadians, from coast to coast. All who are interested in the achievements of Canada's most influential citizens and their significant contributions to the country and the world beyond should acquire this reference title.

Detailed entries give date and place of birth, education, family details, career information, memberships, creative works, honours, languages, and awards, together with full addresses. Included are outstanding Canadians from business, academia, politics, sports, the arts and sciences, etc.

Every year the publisher invites new individuals to complete questionnaires from which new biographies are compiled. The publisher also gives those already listed in earlier editions an opportunity to update their biographies. Those listed are selected because of the positions they hold in Canadian society, or because of the contributions they have made to Canada.

AVAILABLE ONLINE!

Canadian Who's Who is also available online, through Canada's Information Resource Centre (CIRC). Readers can access this title's in-depth and vital networking content in the format that best suits their needs—in print, by subscription or online.

The print edition of *Canadian Who's Who 2024* contains 10,000 entries, while the online edition gives users access to over 27,500 biographies, including all current listings and over 15,800 archived biographies dating back to 1999.

GREY HOUSE PUBLISHING CANADA For more information please contact Grey House Publishing Canada
Tel.: (866)-433-4739 or (416) 644-6479 Fax: (416) 644-1904 | info@greyhouse.ca | www.greyhouse.ca

Canadian Who's Who

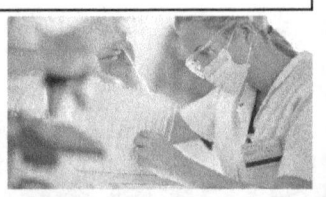

Canadian Who's Who est la seule publication digne de foi de son genre au Canada. Elle donne accès 10 000 dignitaires canadiens de tous les horizons. L'ouvrage annuel rouge vif bien connu, rempli d'information à jour et exacte, est la référence standard en matière de biographies canadiennes contemporaines.

Canadian Who's Who, qui porte sur les réalisations de Canadiens occupant une vaste gamme de postes et de professions, illustre la diversité de la culture canadienne. Ces biographies sont classées en ordre alphabétique et donnent de l'information détaillée sur les réalisations de Canadiens éminents, d'un océan à l'autre. Tous ceux qui s'intéressent aux réalisations des citoyens les plus influents au Canada et à leurs contributions importantes au pays et partout dans le monde doivent se procurer cet ouvrage de référence.

Les entrées détaillées indiquent la date et le lieu de la naissance, traitent de l'éducation, de la famille, de la carrière, des adhésions, des œuvres de création, des distinctions, des langues et des prix - en plus des adresses complètes. Elles comprennent des Canadiens exceptionnels du monde des affaires, des universités, de la politique, des sports, des arts, des sciences et plus encore!

Chaque année, l'éditeur invite de nouvelles personnes à remplir les questionnaires à partir desquels il prépare les nouvelles biographies. Il le remet également aux personnes qui font partie de numéros antérieurs afin de leur permettre d'effectuer une mise à jour. Les personnes retenues le sont en raison des postes qu'elles occupent dans la société canadienne ou de leurs contributions au Canada.

OFFERT EN FORMAT ÉLECTRONIQUE!

Canadian Who's Who est également offert en ligne par l'entremise du Centre de documentation du Canada (CDC). Les lecteurs peuvent accéder au contenu approfondi et essentiel au réseautage de cet ouvrage dans le format qui leur convient le mieux - version imprimée, en ligne ou par abonnement.

L'édition imprimée de *Canadian Who's Who 2024* compte 10 000 entrées tandis qu'en consultant la version en ligne, les utilisateurs ont accès à 27 500 biographies, dont fi ches d'actualité et plus de 15 800 biographies archives qui remontent jusqu'à 1999.

GREY HOUSE PUBLISHING CANADA Pour obtenir plus d'information, veuillez contacter Grey House Publishing Canada
par tél. : 1 866 433-4739 ou 416 644-6479 par téléc. : 416 644-1904 | info@greyhouse.ca | www.greyhouse.ca

Canadian Parliamentary Guide

Your Number One Source for All General Federal Elections Results!

Published annually since before Confederation, the *Canadian Parliamentary Guide* is an indispensable directory, providing biographical information on elected and appointed members in federal and provincial government. Featuring government institutions such as the Governor General's Household, Privy Council and Canadian legislature, this comprehensive collection provides historical and current election results with statistical, provincial and political data.

AVAILABLE IN PRINT AND NOW ONLINE!

THE CANADIAN PARLIAMENTARY GUIDE IS BROKEN DOWN INTO FIVE COMPREHENSIVE CATEGORIES

Monarchy—biographical information on His Majesty King Charles III, The Royal Family and the Governor General

Federal Government—a separate chapter for each of the Privy Council, Senate and House of Commons (including a brief description of the institution, its history in both text and chart format and a list of current members), followed by unparalleled biographical sketches*

General Elections

1867–2019

- information is listed alphabetically by province then by riding name
- notes on each riding include: date of establishment, date of abolition, former division and later divisions, followed by election year and successful candidate's name and party
- by-election information follows

2021

- information for the 2021 election is organized in the same manner but also includes information on all the candidates who ran in each riding, their party affiliation and the number of votes won

Provincial and Territorial Governments—Each provincial chapter includes:

- statistical information
- description of Legislative Assembly
- biographical sketch of the Lieutenant Governor or Commissioner
- list of current Cabinet Members
- dates of legislatures since confederation
- current Members and Constituencies
- biographical sketches*
- general election and by-election results, including the most recent provincial and territorial elections.

Courts: Federal—each court chapter includes a description of the court (Supreme, Federal, Federal Court of Appeal, Court Martial Appeal and Tax Court), its history and a list of its judges followed by biographical sketches*

* Biographical sketches follow a concise yet in-depth format:

Personal Data—place of birth, education, family information

Political Career—political career path and services

Private Career—work history, organization memberships, military history

Available in hardcover print, the *Canadian Parliamentary Guide* is also available electronically via the Web, providing instant access to the government officials you need and the facts you want every time. Use the web version to narrow your search with index fields such as institution, province and name.

Create your own contact lists! Online subscribers can instantly generate their own contact lists and export information into spreadsheets for further use. A great alternative to high cost list broker services!

Photo of the Rt. Hon. Justin Trudeau by Adam Scotti, provided by the Office of the Prime Minister © Her Majesty the Queen in Right of Canada, 2021.

GREY HOUSE PUBLISHING CANADA For more information please contact Grey House Publishing Canada
Tel.: (866)-433-4739 or (416) 644-6479 Fax: (416) 644-1904 | info@greyhouse.ca | www.greyhouse.ca

Guide parlementaire canadien

Votre principale source d'information en matière de résultats d'élections fédérales!

Publié annuellement depuis avant la Confédération, le *Guide parlementaire canadien* est une source fondamentale de notices biographiques des membres élus et nommés aux gouvernements fédéral et provinciaux. Il y est question, notamment, d'établissements gouvernementaux comme la résidence du gouverneur général, le Conseil privé et la législature canadienne. Ce recueil exhaustif présente les résultats historiques et actuels accompagnés de données statistiques, provinciales et politiques.

OFFERT EN FORMAT PAPIER ET DÉSORMAIS ÉLECTRONIQUE!

LE GUIDE PARLEMENTAIRE CANADIEN EST DIVISÉ EN CINQ CATÉGORIES EXHAUSTIVES:

La monarchie—des renseignements biographiques sur Sa Majesté le Roi Charles III, la famille royale et le gouverneur général.

Le gouvernement fédéral—un chapitre distinct pour chacun des sujets suivants: Conseil privé, sénat, Chambre des communes (y compris une brève description de l'institution, son historique sous forme de textes et de graphiques et une liste des membres actuels) suivi de notes biographiques sans pareil.*

Les élections fédérales

1867–2019
- Les renseignements sont présentés en ordre alphabétique par province puis par circonscription.
- Les notes de chaque circonscription comprennent : La date d'établissement, la date d'abolition, l'ancienne circonscription, les circonscriptions ultérieures, etc. puis l'année d'élection ainsi que le nom et le parti des candidats élus.
- Viennent ensuite des renseignements sur l'élection partielle.

2021
- Les renseignements de l'élection 2021 sont organisés de la même manière, mais comprennent également de l'information sur tous les candidats qui se sont présentés dans chaque circonscription, leur appartenance politique et le nombre de voix récoltées.

Gouvernements provinciaux et territoriaux—Chaque chapitre portant sur le gouvernement provincial comprend :
- des renseignements statistiques
- une description de l'Assemblée législative
- des notes biographiques sur le lieutenant-gouverneur ou le commissaire
- une liste des ministres actuels
- les dates de périodes législatives depuis la Confédération
- une liste des membres et des circonscriptions
- des notes biographiques*
- les résultats d'élections générales et partielles, y compris les dernières élections provinciales et territoriales.

Cours : fédérale—chaque chapitre comprend : une description de la cour (suprême, fédérale, cour d'appel fédérale, cour d'appel de la cour martiale et cour de l'impôt), son histoire, une liste des juges qui y siègent ainsi que des notes biographiques.*

* Les notes biographiques respectent un format concis, bien qu'approfondi :

Renseignements personnels—lieu de naissance, formation, renseignements familiaux

Carrière politique—cheminement politique et service public

Carrière privée—antécédents professionnels, membre d'organisations, antécédents militaires

Offert sous couverture rigide ou en format électronique grâce au web, le *Guide parlementaire canadien* donne invariablement un accès instantané aux représentants du gouvernement et aux faits qui font l'objet de vos recherches. Servez-vous de la version en ligne afin de circonscrire vos recherches grâce aux champs spéciaux de l'index comme l'institution, la province et le nom.

Créez vos propres listes! Les abonnés au service en ligne peuvent générer instantanément leurs propres listes de contacts et les exporter en format feuille de calcul pour une utilisation approfondie – une solution de rechange géniale aux services dispendieux d'un commissionnaire en publipostage!

Photo de la très honorable Justin Trudeau par Adam Scotti. Photo fournie par le Bureau du Premier ministre © Sa Majesté la Reine du Chef du Canada, 2021.

GREY HOUSE PUBLISHING CANADA

Pour obtenir plus d'information, veuillez contacter Grey House Publishing Canada
par tél. : 1 866 433-4739 ou 416 644-6479 par téléc. : 416 644-1904 | info@greyhouse.ca | www.greyhouse.ca

Directory of Directors
Your Best Source for Hard-to-Find Business Information

Since 1931, the *Financial Post Directory of Directors* has been recognizing leading Canadian companies and their execs. Today, this title is one of the most comprehensive resources for hard-to-find Canadian business information, allowing readers to access roughly 16,800 executive contacts from Canada's top 1,400 corporations. This prestigious title offers a definitive list of directorships and offices held by noteworthy Canadian business people. It also provides details on leading Canadian companies—publicly traded and privately-owned, including company name, contact information and the names of their executive officers and directors.

ACCESS THE COMPANIES & DIRECTORS YOU NEED IN NO TIME!

The updated 2024 edition of the *Directory of Directors* is jam-packed with information, including:

- **ALL-NEW front matter**: An infographic drawn from data in the book, a report on diversity disclosure practices, reports on what defines a modern board chair and improving boardroom use of technology, and rankings from the FP500.

- **Personal listings**: First name, last name, gender, birth date, degrees, schools attended, executive positions and directorships, previous positions held, main business address and more.

- **Company listings**: Boards of directors and executive officers, head office address, phone and fax numbers, toll-free number, web and email addresses.

Powerful indexes enabling researchers to target just the information they need include:

- An **industrial classification index**: List of key Canadian companies, sorted by industry type according to the Global Industry Classification Standard (GICS®).

- A **geographic location index** grouping all companies in the Company Listings section according to the city and province/state of the head office; and

- An **alphabetical list of abbreviations** providing definitions of common abbreviations used for terms, titles, organizations, honours/fellowships and degrees throughout the Directory.

AVAILABLE ONLINE!

The Directory is also available online, through Canada's Information Resource Centre. Readers can access this title's in-depth and vital networking content in the format that best suits their needs—in print, by subscription or online.

Create your own contact lists! Online subscribers can instantly generate their own contact lists and export information into spreadsheets for further use. A great alternative to high cost list broker services!

GREY HOUSE PUBLISHING CANADA For more information please contact Grey House Publishing Canada
Tel.: (866)-433-4739 or (416) 644-6479 Fax: (416) 644-1904 | info@greyhouse.ca | www.greyhouse.ca

Répertoire des administrateurs

Votre source par excellence de renseignements professionnels difficiles à trouver

Depuis 1931, le Financial Post Directory of Directors (Répertoire des administrateurs du Financial Post) reconnaît les sociétés canadiennes importantes et leur haute direction. De nos jours, cet ouvrage compte parmi certaines des ressources les plus exhaustives lorsqu'il est question des renseignements d'affaires canadiens difficiles à trouver. Il permet aux lecteurs d'accéder à environ 16 800 coordonnées d'administrateurs provenant des 1 400 sociétés les plus importantes au Canada. Ce document prestigieux comprend une liste définitive des postes d'administrateurs et des fonctions que ces gens d'affaires canadiens remarquables occupent. Il offre également des détails sur des sociétés canadiennes importantes – privées ou négociées sur le marché – y compris le nom de l'entreprise, ses coordonnées et le nombre des membres de sa haute direction et de ses administrateurs.

UN ACCÈS RAPIDE ET FACILE À TOUS LES ENTREPRISES ET DIRECTEURS DONT VOUS AVEZ BESOIN!

La version mise à jour de 2024 du Répertoire des administrateurs du Financial Post est remplie d'information, notamment:

- **NOUVELLE section de textes préliminaires** –une infographie inspirée des données de l'ouvrage; un rapport sur les pratiques de divulgation de la diversité; des rapports sur ce qui définit un président de conseil d'administration moderne et l'amélioration de l'utilisation de la technologie dans les conseils d'administration; le classement le plus récent au FP500.
- **Données personnelles** – prénom, nom de famille, sexe, date de naissance, diplômes, écoles fréquentées, poste de cadre et d'administrateur, postes occupés préalablement, adresse professionnelle principale et plus encore.
- **Listes de sociétés** – conseils d'administration et cadres supérieurs, adresse du siège social, numéros de téléphone et de télécopieur, numéro sans frais, adresse électronique et site Web.

Des index puissants permettent aux utilisateurs de cibler l'information dont ils ont besoin, notamment:

- **Index de classement industriel** - énumère les sociétés classées par type d'industrie général selon le Global Industry Classification Standard (GICS^{MD}).
- l'**Index des emplacements géographiques** qui comprend toutes les sociétés de la section Liste des sociétés en fonction de la ville et de la province/de l'état où se trouve le siège social;
- une **liste des abréviations en ordre alphabétique** définit les abréviations courantes pour la terminologie, les titres, les organisations, les distinctions/fellowships et les diplômes mentionnés dans le Répertoire.

OFFERT EN FORMAT ÉLECTRONIQUE!

Le Répertoire est également accessible en ligne par l'entremise du Centre de documentation du Canada. Les lecteurs peuvent accéder au contenu approfondi et essentiel au réseautage de cet ouvrage dans le format qui leur convient le mieux - version imprimée, en ligne ou par abonnement.

Créez vos propres listes! Les abonnés au service en ligne peuvent générer instantanément leurs propres listes de contacts et les exporter en format feuille de calcul pour une utilisation approfondie – une solution de rechange géniale aux services dispendieux d'un commissionnaire en publipostage.

GREY HOUSE PUBLISHING CANADA

Pour obtenir plus d'information, veuillez contacter Grey House Publishing Canada
par tél. : 1 866 433-4739 ou 416 644-6479 par téléc. : 416 644-1904 | info@greyhouse.ca | www.greyhouse.ca

Associations Canada
Makes Researching Organizations Quick and Easy

Associations Canada is an easy-to-use compendium, providing detailed indexes, listings and abstracts on over 20,500 local, regional, provincial, national and international organizations (identifying location, budget, founding date, management, scope of activity and funding source—just to name a few).

POWERFUL INDEXES HELP YOU TARGET THE ORGANIZATIONS YOU WANT

There are a number of criteria you can use to target specific organizations. Organized with the user in mind, *Associations Canada* is broken down into a number of indexes to help you find what you're looking for quickly and easily.

- **Subject Index**—listing of Canadian and foreign association headquarters, alphabetically by subject and keyword
- **Acronym Index**—an alphabetical listing of acronyms and corresponding Canadian and foreign associations, in both official languages
- **Budget Index**—Canadian associations, alphabetical within eight budget categories
- **Conferences & Conventions Index**—meetings sponsored by Canadian and foreign associations, listed alphabetically by conference name
- **Executive Name Index**—alphabetical listing of key contacts of Canadian associations, for both headquarters and branches
- **Geographic Index**—listing of headquarters, branch offices, chapters and divisions of Canadian associations, alphabetical within province and city
- **Mailing List Index**—associations that offer mailing lists, alphabetical by subject
- **Registered Charitable Organizations Index**—listing of associations that are registered charities, alphabetical by subject

PRINT OR ONLINE – QUICK AND EASY ACCESS TO ALL THE INFORMATION YOU NEED!

Available in softcover print or electronically via the web, *Associations Canada* provides instant access to the people you need and the facts you want every time. Whereas the print edition is verified and updated annually, ongoing changes are added to the web version on a regular basis. The web version allows you to narrow your search by using index fields such as name or type of organization, subject, location, contact name or title and postal code.

Create your own contact lists! Online subscribers have the option to instantly generate their own contact lists and export them into spreadsheets for further use—a great alternative to high cost list broker services.

ASSOCIATIONS CANADA PROVIDES COMPLETE ACCESS TO THESE HIGHLY LUCRATIVE MARKETS:

Travel & Tourism
- Who's hosting what event...when and where?
- Check on events up to three years in advance

Journalism and Media
- Pure research—What do they do? Who is in charge? What's their budget?
- Check facts and sources in one step

Libraries
- Refer researchers to the most complete Canadian association reference anywhere

Business
- Target your market, research your interests, compile profiles and identify membership lists
- Warm up your cold calls with all the background you need to sell your product or service
- Preview prospects by budget, market interest or geographic location

Association Executives
- Look for strategic alliances with associations of similar interest
- Spot opportunities or conflicts with convention plans

Research & Government
- Scan interest groups or identify charities in your area of concern
- Check websites, publications and speaker availability
- Evaluate mandates, affiliations and scope

GREY HOUSE PUBLISHING CANADA For more information please contact Grey House Publishing Canada
Tel.: (866)-433-4739 or (416) 644-6479 Fax: (416) 644-1904 | info@greyhouse.ca | www.greyhouse.ca

Associations du Canada
La recherche d'organisations simplifiée

Il s'agit d'un recueil facile d'utilisation qui offre des index, des fiches descriptives et des résumés exhaustifs de plus de 20 500 organismes locaux, régionaux, provinciaux, nationaux et internationaux. Il donne, entre autres, des détails sur leur emplacement, leur budget, leur date de mise sur pied, l'éventail de leurs activités et leurs sources de financement.

En plus d'affecter plus d'un milliard de dollars annuellement aux frais de transport, à la participation à des congrès et à la mise en marché, *Associations du Canada* débourse des millions de dollars dans sa quête pour répondre aux intérêts de ses membres.

DES INDEX PUISSANTS QUI VOUS AIDENT À CIBLER LES ORGANISATIONS VOULUES

Vous pouvez vous servir de plusieurs critères pour cibler des organisations précises. C'est avec l'utilisateur en tête qu'*Associations du Canada* a été divisé en plusieurs index pour vous aider à trouver, rapidement et facilement, ce que vous cherchez.

- **Index des sujets**—liste des sièges sociaux d'associations canadiennes et étrangères; sujets classés en ordre alphabétique et mot-clé.
- **Index des acronymes**—liste alphabétique des acronymes et des associations canadiennes et étrangères équivalentes; présenté dans les deux langues officielles.
- **Index des budgets**—associations canadiennes classées en ordre alphabétique parmi huit catégories de budget.
- **Index des congrès**—rencontres commanditées par des associations canadiennes et étrangères; classées en ordre alphabétique selon le titre de l'événement.
- **Index des directeurs**—liste alphabétique des principales personnes-ressources des associations canadiennes, aux sièges sociaux et aux succursales.
- **Index géographique**—liste des sièges sociaux, des succursales, des sections régionales et des divisions des associations canadiennes; ordre alphabétique au sein des provinces et des villes.
- **Index des listes de distribution**—liste des associations qui offrent des listes de distribution; en ordre alphabétique selon le sujet.
- **Index des œuvres de bienfaisance enregistrées**—liste des associations enregistrées en tant qu'œuvres de bienfaisance; en ordre alphabétique selon le sujet.

OFFERT EN FORMAT PAPIER OU EN LIGNE—UN ACCÈS RAPIDE ET FACILE À TOUS LES RENSEIGNEMENTS DONT VOUS AVEZ BESOIN!

Offert sous couverture souple ou en format électronique grâce au web, *Associations du Canada* donne invariablement un accès instantané aux personnes et aux faits dont vous avez besoin. Si la version imprimée est vérifiée et mise à jour annuellement, des changements continus sont apportés mensuellement à la base de données en ligne. Servez-vous de la version en ligne afin de circonscrire vos recherches grâce à des champs spéciaux de l'index comme le nom de l'organisation ou son type, le sujet, l'emplacement, le nom de la personne-ressource ou son titre et le code postal.

Créez vos propres listes! Les abonnés au service en ligne peuvent générer instantanément leurs propres listes de contacts et les exporter en format feuille de calcul pour une utilisation approfondie – une solution de rechange géniale aux services dispendieux d'un commissionnaire en publipostage.

ASSOCIATIONS DU CANADA OFFRE UN ACCÈS COMPLET À CES MARCHÉS HAUTEMENT LUCRATIFS

Voyage et tourisme
- Renseignez-vous sur les hôtes des évènements, sur les dates et les endroits.
- Consultez les évènements trois ans au préalable.

Journalisme et médias
- Recherche authentique—quel est leur centre d'activité? Qui est la personne responsable? Quel est leur budget?
- Vérifiez les faits et sources en une seule étape.

Bibliothèques
- Orientez les chercheurs vers la référence la plus complète en ce qui concerne les associations canadiennes.

Commerce
- Ciblez votre marché, faites une recherche selon vos sujets de prédilection, compilez des profils et recensez des listes des membres.
- Préparez votre sollicitation au hasard en obtenant les renseignements dont vous avez besoin pour offrir votre produit ou service.
- Obtenez un aperçu de vos clients potentiels selon les budgets, les intérêts au marché ou l'emplacement géographique.

Directeurs d'associations
- Recherchez des alliances stratégiques avec des associations partageant vos intérêts.
- Repérez des occasions ou des conflits dans le cadre de la planification des congrès.

Recherche et gouvernement
- Parcourez les groupes d'intérêts ou identifiez les organismes de bienfaisance de votre domaine d'intérêt.
- Consultez les sites Web, les publications et vérifiez la disponibilité des conférenciers.
- Évaluez les mandats, les affiliations et le champ d'application.

GREY HOUSE PUBLISHING CANADA

Pour obtenir plus d'information, veuillez contacter Grey House Publishing Canada
par tél. : 1 866 433-4739 ou 416 644-6479 par téléc. : 416 644-1904 | info@greyhouse.ca | www.greyhouse.ca

Canadian Environmental Resource Guide
The Only Complete Guide to the Business of Environmental Management

The *Canadian Environmental Resource Guide* provides data on every aspect of the environment industry in unprecedented detail. It's one-stop searching for details on government offices and programs, information sources, product and service firms and trade fairs that pertain to the business of environmental management. All information is fully indexed and cross-referenced for easy use. The directory features current information and key contacts in Canada's environmental industry including:

ENVIRONMENTAL UP-DATE
- Information on prominent environmentalists, environmental abbreviations and a summary of recent environmental events
- Updated articles, rankings, statistics and charts on all aspects of the environmental industry
- Trade shows, conferences and seminars for the current year and beyond

ENVIRONMENTAL INDUSTRY RESOURCES
- Comprehensive listings for companies and firms producing and selling products and services in the environmental sector, including markets served, working language and percentage of revenue sources: public and private
- Environmental law firms, with lawyers' areas of speciality
- Detailed indexes by subject, geography and ISO

ENVIRONMENTAL GOVERNMENT LISTINGS
- Information on important intergovernmental offices and councils, and listings of environmental trade representatives abroad
- In-depth listings of environmental information at the municipal level, including population and number of households, water and waste treatment, landfill statistics and special by-laws and bans, as well as key environmental contacts for each municipality

Available in softcover print or electronically via the web, the *Canadian Environmental Resource Guide* provides instant access to the people you need and the facts you want every time. The *Canadian Environmental Resource Guide* is verified and updated annually. Ongoing changes are added to the web version on a regular basis.

CANADIAN ENVIRONMENTAL RESOURCE GUIDE OFFERS EVEN MORE CONTENT ONLINE!

Environmental Information Resources—Extensive listings of special libraries and thousands of environmental associations, with information on membership, environmental activities, key contacts and more.

Government Listings—Every federal and provincial department and agency influencing environmental initiatives and purchasing policies.

The web version allows you to narrow your search by using index fields such as name or type of organization, subject, location, contact name or title and postal code.

Create your own contact lists! Online subscribers have the option to instantly generate their own contact lists and export them into spreadsheets for further use—a great alternative to high cost list broker services.

GREY HOUSE PUBLISHING CANADA For more information please contact Grey House Publishing Canada
Tel.: (866)-433-4739 or (416) 644-6479 Fax: (416) 644-1904 | info@greyhouse.ca | www.greyhouse.ca

Guide des ressources environnementales canadiennes
Le seul guide complet dédié à la gestion de l'environnement

Le *Guide des ressources environnementales canadiennes* offre de l'information relative à tous les aspects de l'industrie de l'environnement dans les moindres détails. Il permet d'effectuer une recherche de données complètes sur les bureaux et programmes gouvernementaux, les sources de renseignements, les entreprises de produits et de services et les foires commerciales qui portent sur les activités de la gestion de l'environnement. Toute l'information est entièrement indexée et effectue un double renvoi pour une consultation facile. Le répertoire présente des renseignements actualisés et les personnes-ressources clés de l'industrie de l'environnement au Canada, y compris les suivants.

MISE À JOUR SUR L'INDUSTRIE DE L'ENVIRONNEMENT

- De l'information sur d'éminents environnementalistes, les abréviations utilisées dans le domaine de l'environnement et un résumé des événements environnementaux récents
- Des articles, des classements, des statistiques et des graphiques mis à jour sur tous les aspects de l'industrie verte
- Les salons professionnels, conférences et séminaires qui ont lieu cette année et ceux qui sont prévus

RESSOURCES DE L'INDUSTRIE ENVIRONNEMENTALE

- Des listes exhaustives des entreprises et des cabinets qui fabriquent ou offrent des produits et des services dans le domaine de l'environnement, y compris les marchés desservis, la langue de travail et la ventilation des sources de revenus – publics et privés
- Une liste complète des cabinets spécialisés en droit environnemental
- Des index selon le sujet, la géographie et la certification ISO

LISTES GOUVERNEMENTALES RELATIVES À L'ENVIRONNEMENT

- De l'information sur les bureaux et conseils intergouvernementaux importants ainsi que des listes des représentants de l'éco-commerce à l'extérieur du pays
- Des listes approfondies portant sur de l'information environnementale au palier municipal, notamment la population et le nombre de ménages, le traitement de l'eau et des déchets, des statistiques sur les décharges, des règlements et des interdictions spéciaux ainsi que des personnes-ressources clés en environnement pour chaque municipalité

Offert sous couverture rigide ou en format électronique grâce au Web, le *Guide des ressources environnementales canadiennes* offre invariablement un accès instantané aux représentants du gouvernement et aux faits qui font l'objet de vos recherches. Il est vérifié et mis à jour annuellement. La version en ligne est mise à jour mensuellement.

LE GUIDE DES RESSOURCES ENVIRONNEMENTALES CANADIENNES DONNE ACCÈS À PLUS DE CONTENU EN LIGNE!

Des ressources informationnelles sur l'environnement—Des bibliothèques et des centres de ressources spécialisés, et des milliers d'associations environnementales, avec de l'information sur l'adhésion, les activités environnementales, les personnes-ressources principales et plus encore.

Listes gouvernementales—Toutes les agences et tous les services gouvernementaux fédéraux et provinciaux qui exercent une influence sur les initiatives en matière d'environnement et de politiques d'achat.

Servez-vous de la version en ligne afin de circonscrire vos recherches grâce à des champs spéciaux de l'index comme le nom de l'organisation ou son type, le sujet, l'emplacement, le nom de la personne-ressource ou son titre et le code postal.

Créez vos propres listes! Les abonnés au service en ligne peuvent générer instantanément leurs propres listes de contacts et les exporter en format feuille de calcul pour une utilisation approfondie—une solution de rechange géniale aux services dispendieux d'un commissionnaire en publipostage.

GREY HOUSE PUBLISHING CANADA

Pour obtenir plus d'information, veuillez contacter Grey House Publishing Canada
par tél. : 1 866 433-4739 ou 416 644-6479 par téléc. : 416 644-1904 | info@greyhouse.ca | www.greyhouse.ca

Libraries Canada
Gain Access to Complete and Detailed Information on Canadian Libraries

Libraries Canada brings together the most current information from across the entire Canadian library sector, including libraries and branch libraries, educational libraries, regional systems, resource centres, archives, related periodicals, library schools and programs, provincial and governmental agencies and associations.

As the nation's leading library directory for over 35 years, *Libraries Canada* gives you access to almost 10,000 names and addresses of contacts in these institutions. Also included are valuable details such as library symbol, number of staff, operating systems, library type and acquisitions budget, hours of operation—all thoroughly indexed and easy to find.

INSTANT ACCESS TO CANADIAN LIBRARY SECTOR INFORMATION
Developed for publishers, advocacy groups, computer hardware suppliers, internet service providers and other diverse groups which provide products and services to the library community; associations that need to maintain a current list of library resources in Canada; and research departments, students and government agencies which require information about the types of services and programs available at various research institutions, *Libraries Canada* will help you find the information you need—quickly and easily.

EXPERT SEARCH OPTIONS AVAILABLE WITH ONLINE VERSION...
Available in print and online, *Libraries Canada* delivers easily accessible, quality information that has been verified and organized for easy retrieval. Five easy-to-use indexes assist you in navigating the print edition while the online version utilizes multiple index fields that help you get results.

Available on Grey House Publishing Canada's CIRC interface, you can choose between Keyword and Advanced search to pinpoint information. Designed for both novice and advanced researchers, you can conduct simple text searches as well as powerful Boolean searches, plus you can narrow your search by using index fields such as name or type of institution, headquarters, location, area code, contact name or title and postal code. Save your searches to build on at a later date or use the mark record function to view, print, e-mail or export your selected records.

Online subscribers have the option to instantly generate their own contact lists and export them into spreadsheets for further use. A great alternative to high cost list broker services.

LIBRARIES CANADA GIVES YOU ALL THE ESSENTIALS FOR EACH INSTITUTION:

Name, address, contact information, key personnel, number of staff

Collection information, type of library, acquisitions budget, subject area, special collection

User services, number of branches, hours of operation, ILL information, photocopy and microform facilities, for-fee research, Internet access

Systems information, details on electronic access, operating and online systems, Internet and e-mail software, Internet connectivity, access to electronic resources

Additional information including associations, publications and regional systems

With almost 60% of the data changing annually it has never been more important to have the latest version of *Libraries Canada*.

GREY HOUSE PUBLISHING CANADA
For more information please contact Grey House Publishing Canada
Tel.: (866) 433-4739 or (416) 644-6479 Fax: (416) 644-1904 | info@greyhouse.ca | www.greyhouse.ca

Bibliothèques Canada

Accédez aux renseignements complets et détaillés au sujet des bibliothèques canadiennes

Bibliothèques Canada combine les renseignements les plus à jour provenant du secteur des bibliothèques de partout au Canada, y compris les bibliothèques et leurs succursales, les bibliothèques éducatives, les systèmes régionaux, les centres de ressources, les archives, les périodiques pertinents, les écoles de bibliothéconomie et leurs programmes, les organismes provinciaux et gouvernementaux ainsi que les associations.

Principal répertoire des bibliothèques depuis plus de 35 ans, *Bibliothèques Canada* vous donne accès à près de 10 000 noms et adresses de personnes-ressources pour ces établissements. Il comprend également des détails précieux comme le symbole d'identification de bibliothèque, le nombre de membres du personnel, les systèmes d'exploitation, le type de bibliothèque et le budget attribué aux acquisitions, les heures d'ouverture – autant d'information minutieusement indexée et facile à trouver.

Offert en version imprimée et en ligne, *Bibliothèques Canada* offre des renseignements de qualité, facile d'accès, qui ont été vérifiés et organisés afin de les obtenir facilement. Cinq index conviviaux vous aident dans la navigation du numéro imprimé tandis que la version en ligne vous permet de saisir plusieurs champs d'index pour vous aider à découvrir l'information voulue.

ACCÈS INSTANTANÉ AUX RENSEIGNEMENTS DU DOMAINE DES BIBLIOTHÈQUES CANADIENNES

Conçu pour les éditeurs, les groupes de revendication, les fournisseurs de matériel informatique, les fournisseurs de services Internet et autres groupes qui offrent produits et services aux bibliothèques; les associations qui ont besoin de conserver une liste à jour des ressources bibliothécaires au Canada; les services de recherche, les organismes étudiants et gouvernementaux qui ont besoin d'information au sujet des types de services et de programmes offerts par divers établissements de recherche, *Bibliothèques Canada* vous aide à trouver l'information nécessaire – rapidement et simplement.

LA VERSION EN LIGNE COMPREND DES OPTIONS DE RECHERCHE POUSSÉES...

À partir de l'interface du Centre de documentation du Canada de Grey House Publishing Canada, vous pouvez choisir entre la recherche poussée et rapide pour cibler votre information. Vous pouvez effectuer des recherches par texte simple, conçues à la fois pour les chercheurs débutants et chevronnés, ainsi que des recherches booléennes puissantes. Vous pouvez également restreindre votre recherche à l'aide des champs d'index, comme le nom ou le type d'établissement, le siège social, l'emplacement, l'indicatif régional, le nom de la personne-ressource ou son titre et le code postal. Enregistrez vos recherches pour vous en servir plus tard ou utilisez la fonction de marquage pour afficher, imprimer, envoyer par courriel ou exporter les dossiers sélectionnés.

Les abonnés au service en ligne peuvent générer instantanément leurs propres listes de contacts et les exporter en format feuille de calcul pour une utilisation approfondie – une solution de rechange géniale aux services dispendieux d'un commissionnaire en publipostage.

BIBLIOTHÈQUES CANADA VOUS DONNE TOUS LES RENSEIGNEMENTS ESSENTIELS RELATIFS À CHAQUE ÉTABLISSEMENT :

Leurs nom et adresse, les coordonnées de la personne-ressource, les membres clés du personnel, le nombre de membres du personnel

L'information relative aux collections, le type de bibliothèque, le budget attribué aux acquisitions, le domaine, les collections particulières

Les services aux utilisateurs, le nombre de succursales, les heures d'ouverture, les renseignements relatifs au PEB, les services de photocopie et de microforme, la recherche rémunérée, l'accès à Internet

L'information relative aux systèmes, des détails sur l'accès électronique, les systèmes d'exploitation et ceux en ligne, Internet et le logiciel de messagerie électronique, la connectivité à Internet, l'accès aux ressources électroniques

L'information supplémentaire, y compris les associations, les publications et les systèmes régionaux

Alors que près de 60 % des données sont modifiées annuellement, il est plus important que jamais de posséder la plus récente version de *Bibliothèques Canada*.

GREY HOUSE PUBLISHING CANADA Pour obtenir plus d'information, veuillez contacter Grey House Publishing Canada
par tél. : 1 866 433-4739 ou 416 644-6479 par téléc. : 416 644-1904 | info@greyhouse.ca | www.greyhouse.ca

Financial Services Canada
Unparalleled Coverage of the Canadian Financial Service Industry

With corporate listings for over **30,000** organizations and hard-to-find business information, *Financial Services Canada* is the most up-to-date source for names and contact numbers of industry professionals, senior executives, portfolio managers, financial advisors, agency bureaucrats and elected representatives.

Financial Services Canada is the definitive resource for detailed listings—providing valuable contact information including: name, title, organization, profile, associated companies, telephone and fax numbers, e-mail and website addresses. Use our online database and refine your search by stock symbol, revenue, year founded, assets, ownership type or number of employees.

POWERFUL INDEXES HELP YOU LOCATE THE CRUCIAL FINANCIAL INFORMATION YOU NEED.

Organized with the user in mind, *Financial Services Canada* contains categorized listings and 4 easy-to-use indexes:

- **Alphabetic**—financial organizations listed in alphabetical sequence by company name
- **Geographic**—financial institutions broken down by town or city
- **Executive Name**—all officers, directors and senior personnel in alphabetical order by surname
- **Insurance class**—lists all companies by insurance type

Reduce the time you spend compiling lists, researching company information and searching for e-mail addresses. Whether you are interested in contacting a finance lawyer regarding international and domestic joint ventures, need to generate a list of foreign banks in Canada or want to contact the Toronto Stock Exchange—*Financial Services Canada* gives you the power to find all the data you need.

PRINT OR ONLINE – QUICK AND EASY ACCESS TO ALL THE INFORMATION YOU NEED!

Available in softcover print or electronically via the web, *Financial Services Canada* provides instant access to the people you need and the facts you want every time.

Financial Services Canada print edition is verified and updated annually. Ongoing changes are added to the web version on a regular basis. The web version allows you to narrow your search by using index fields such as name or type of organization, subject, location, contact name or title and postal code.

Create your own contact lists! Online subscribers have the option to instantly generate their own contact lists and export them into spreadsheets for further use—a great alternative to high cost list broker services.

ACCESS TO CURRENT LISTINGS FOR...

Banks and Depository Institutions
- Domestic and savings banks
- Foreign banks and branches
- Foreign bank representative offices
- Trust companies
- Credit unions

Non-Depository Institutions
- Bond rating companies
- Collection agencies
- Credit card companies
- Financing and loan companies
- Trustees in bankruptcy

Investment Management Firms, including securities and commodities
- Financial planning / investment management companies
- Investment dealers
- Investment fund companies
- Pension/money management companies
- Stock exchanges
- Holding companies

Insurance Companies, including federal and provincial
- Reinsurance companies
- Fraternal benefit societies
- Mutual benefit companies
- Reciprocal exchanges

Accounting and Law
- Accountants
- Actuary consulting firms
- Law firms (specializing in finance)

Major Canadian Companies
- Key financial contacts for public, private and Crown corporations

Associations
- Associations and institutes serving the financial services sector

Financial Technology & Services
- Companies involved in financial software and other technical areas.

Access even more content online:
Government and Publications
- Federal, provincial and territorial contacts
- Leading publications serving the financial services industry

---

GREY HOUSE PUBLISHING CANADA For more information please contact Grey House Publishing Canada
Tel.: (866)-433-4739 or (416) 644-6479 Fax: (416) 644-1904 | info@greyhouse.ca | www.greyhouse.ca

Services financiers au Canada

Une couverture sans pareille de l'industrie des services financiers canadiens

Grâce à plus de 30 000 organisations et renseignements commerciaux rares, *Services financiers du Canada* est la source la plus à jour de noms et de coordonnées de professionnels, de membres de la haute direction, de gestionnaires de portefeuille, de conseillers financiers, de fonctionnaires et de représentants élus de l'industrie.

Services financiers du Canada intègre les plus récentes modifications à l'industrie afin de vous offrir les détails les plus à jour au sujet de chaque entreprise, notamment le nom, le titre, l'organisation, les numéros de téléphone et de télécopieur, le courriel et l'adresse du site Web. Servez-vous de la base de données en ligne et raffinez votre recherche selon le symbole, le revenu, l'année de création, les immobilisations, le type de propriété ou le nombre d'employés.

DES INDEX PUISSANTS VOUS AIDENT À TROUVER LES RENSEIGNEMENTS FINANCIERS ESSENTIELS DONT VOUS AVEZ BESOIN.

C'est avec l'utilisateur en tête que Services financiers au Canada a été conçu; il contient des listes catégorisées et quatre index faciles d'utilisation :

Alphabétique—les organisations financières apparaissent en ordre alphabétique, selon le nom de l'entreprise.

Géographique—les institutions financières sont détaillées par ville.

Nom de directeur—tous les agents, directeurs et cadres supérieurs sont classés en ordre alphabétique, selon leur nom de famille.

Classe d'assurance—toutes les entreprises selon leur type d'assurance.

Passez moins de temps à préparer des listes, à faire des recherches ou à chercher des contacts et des courriels. Que vous soyez intéressé à contacter un avocat en droit des affaires au sujet de projets conjoints internationaux et nationaux, que vous ayez besoin de générer une liste des banques étrangères au Canada ou que vous souhaitiez communiquer avec la Bourse de Toronto, *Services financiers au Canada* vous permet de trouver toutes les données dont vous avez besoin.

OFFERT EN FORMAT PAPIER OU EN LIGNE – UN ACCÈS RAPIDE ET FACILE À TOUS LES RENSEIGNEMENTS DONT VOUS AVEZ BESOIN!

Offert sous couverture rigide ou en format électronique grâce au Web, Services financiers du Canada donne invariablement un accès instantané aux personnes et aux faits dont vous avez besoin. Si la version imprimée est vérifiée et mise à jour annuellement, des changements continus sont apportés mensuellement à la base de données en ligne. Servez-vous de la version en ligne afin de circonscrire vos recherches grâce à des champs spéciaux de l'index comme le nom de l'organisation ou son type, le sujet, l'emplacement, le nom de la personne-ressource ou son titre et le code postal.

Créez vos propres listes! Les abonnés au service en ligne peuvent générer instantanément leurs propres listes de contacts et les exporter en format feuille de calcul pour une utilisation approfondie – une solution de rechange géniale aux services dispendieux d'un commissionnaire en publipostage.

ACCÉDEZ AUX LISTES ACTUELLES...

Banques et institutions de dépôt
- Banques nationales et d'épargne
- Banques étrangères et leurs succursales
- Bureaux des représentants de banques étrangères
- Sociétés de fiducie
- Coopératives d'épargne et de crédit

Établissements financiers
- Entreprises de notation des obligations
- Agences de placement
- Compagnies de carte de crédit
- Sociétés de financement et de prêt
- Syndics de faillite

Sociétés de gestion de placements, y compris les valeurs et marchandises
- Entreprises de planification financière et de gestion des investissements
- Maisons de courtage de valeurs
- Courtiers en épargne collective
- Entreprises de gestion de la pension/de trésorerie
- Bourses
- Sociétés de portefeuille

Compagnies d'assurance, fédérales et provinciales
- Compagnies de réassurance
- Sociétés fraternelles
- Sociétés de secours mutuel
- Échanges selon la formule de réciprocité

Comptabilité et droit
- Comptables
- Cabinets d'actuaires-conseils
- Cabinets d'avocats (spécialisés en finance)

Principales entreprises canadiennes
- Principaux contacts financiers pour les sociétés de capitaux publiques, privées et de la Couronne

Les associations et Technologie et services financiers

Accès à plus de contenu en ligne: Gouvernement et Publications
- Personnes-ressources aux paliers fédéral, provincial et territoriaux
- Principales publications qui desservent l'industrie des services financiers

---

GREY HOUSE PUBLISHING CANADA

Pour obtenir plus d'information, veuillez contacter Grey House Publishing Canada
par tél. : 1 866 433-4739 ou 416 644-6479 par téléc. : 416 644-1904 | info@greyhouse.ca | www.greyhouse.ca

Careers & Employment Canada

Careers & Employment Canada is the go-to resource for job-seekers across Canada, with detailed, current information on everything from industry associations to summer job opportunities. Divided into five helpful sections, this guide contains 10,000 organizations and 20,000 industry contacts to aid in research and jump-start careers in a variety of fields.

ADDITIONAL RESOURCES INCLUDE:

- **Associations**
- **Employers**
    - Arts & Culture
    - Business & Finance
    - Education
    - Environmental
    - Government
    - Healthcare
    - Legal
    - Major Corporations in Canada
    - Telecommunications & Media
    - Transportation
- **Recruiters**
- **Summer Jobs**
- **Career & Employment Websites**
    - National & Regional
    - Industry
    - Topic-Specific
    - Employment Options
    - Clientele
    - Where to Get Resources

AVAILABLE ONLINE!

This content is also available online on Canada's Information Resource Centre (CIRC), where users can search, sort, save and export the thousands of listings available. Please visit www.greyhouse.ca to sign up for a free trial.

Rounding off this guide are 70 pages of reports on the current job market in Canada, a list of industry Awards and Honours, as well as Entry, Executive, and Government Contact indexes for even easier reference. Valuable for employment professionals, librarians, teachers, and job-seekers alike, *Careers & Employment Canada* helps take the strain out of job searching by providing a direct link to the organizations and contacts that matter most.

A CLOSER LOOK AT WHAT'S INSIDE:

Reports on the Job Market—A series of articles on the current job market sourced from Statistics Canada—everything from equity in the workplace to the many ways in which the COVID-19 pandemic has affected the labour market.

Associations—Nearly 800 national associations covering an array of industries and professions.

Employers—Need-to-know companies and organizations broken down into 11 master categories such as Arts & Culture, Education, Government, and Telecommunications & Media.

Recruiters—Top recruiting firms across Canada, organized by national and provincial scope.

Summer Jobs—National and regional summer job opportunities—everything from government agencies to summer camps

Career & Employment Websites—Includes hiring and job board platforms broken down by industry, employment tools, and resources by job type and specialized clientele such as Indigenous, New Canadians, People with Disabilities, Women, and Youth.

GREY HOUSE PUBLISHING CANADA For more information please contact Grey House Publishing Canada
Tel.: (866)-433-4739 or (416) 644-6479 Fax: (416) 644-1904 | info@greyhouse.ca | www.greyhouse.ca

Carrières et emploi Canada

Carrières et emploi Canada est la ressource privilégiée pour les personnes en recherche d'emploi partout au Canada. Elle contient de l'information détaillée et actuelle, des associations de l'industrie aux offres d'emploi d'été. Divisé en cinq sections pratiques, ce guide comprend 10 000 contacts d'organisations et 20 000 d'industrie pour aider à la recherche d'emploi et démarrer des carrières dans divers domaines.

LES RESSOURCES SUPPLÉMENTAIRES COMPRENNENT :

- **Associations**
- **Employeurs**
  - Arts et culture
  - Affaires et finances
  - Formation
  - Environnement
  - Gouvernement
  - Soins de santé
  - Domaine juridique
  - Grandes entreprises au Canada
  - Télécommunications et médias
  - Transport
- **Recruteurs**
- **Emplois d'été**
- **Sites sur les carrières et l'emploi**
  - À l'échelle nationale et régionale
  - Industrie
  - Relatif à un sujet précis
  - Possibilités d'emploi
  - Communauté
  - Où trouver les ressources

OFFERT EN LIGNE!

Ce contenu est également offert en ligne sur le centre de documentation du Canada (CIRC) où les utilisateurs peuvent effectuer des recherches, trier, sauvegarder et exporter des milliers d'entrées disponibles. Veuillez visiter www.greyhouse.ca (en anglais uniquement) pour vous inscrire afin d'en faire un essai gratuit.

À la fin de ce guide, vous trouverez 70 pages de rapports sur le marché de l'emploi actuel au Canada, une liste des prix remis par l'industrie ainsi que des index classés par entrée, direction et contact gouvernemental pour en faciliter davantage la consultation. Outil précieux pour les professionnels de l'emploi, bibliothécaires, enseignants et chercheurs d'emplois, *Carrières et emploi Canada* aide à alléger la recherche d'emploi en offrant un lien direct avec les organisations et personnes-ressources plus essentielles que jamais.

UN EXAMEN PLUS APPROFONDI DU CONTENU :

Rapports sur le marché de l'emploi—Une série d'articles sur le marché du travail actuel provenant de Statistiques Canada : de l'équité en milieu de travail aux divers impacts de la pandémie de la COVID-19 sur le marché de l'emploi.

Associations—Près de 800 associations nationales portant sur une gamme d'industries et de professions.

Employeurs—Les entreprises et organisations essentielles, divisées en 11 catégories principales comme les arts et la culture, l'éducation, le gouvernement, les télécommunications et les médias.

Recruteurs—Les principales agences de recrutement partout au Canada, selon leur portée nationale et provinciale.

Emplois d'été—Les occasions d'emploi d'été, à l'échelle nationale et régionale; des agences gouvernementales aux camps d'été.

Sites Web professionnels et d'emplois—Comprend les plateformes d'embauche et d'offres d'emploi, divisées par industrie, outils d'embauche et les ressources par type d'emploi et communautés précises, notamment les Autochtones, nouveaux Canadiens, personnes handicapées, femmes et jeunes.

GREY HOUSE PUBLISHING CANADA

Pour obtenir plus d'information, veuillez contacter Grey House Publishing Canada
par tél. : 1 866 433-4739 ou 416 644-6479 par téléc. : 416 644-1904 | info@greyhouse.ca | www.greyhouse.ca

Cannabis Canada

Cannabis Canada is a one-of-a-kind resource covering all aspects of this growing industry. Featuring a wide-ranging collection of reports and statistics, you'll find everything you need to know about this now-legal marketplace, including need-to-know international information.

This first edition includes the State of the Cannabis Industry 2019, exploring the history of marijuana, current regulations, insightful reports, and listings of upcoming trade shows and conferences.

Readers will also discover the brand new Cannabis Industry Buyer's Guide, featuring everything from Licensed Producers to consulting firms, equipment manufacturers to security firms, and more. All listings include specialized fields that go far beyond name and address, and boast crucial, current key contacts.

ADDITIONAL RESOURCES INCLUDE:

- Industry associations
- Financial and venture capital firms
- Law firms
- Government agencies
- Post-secondary schools
- Healthcare and treatment facilities
- Publications

Rounding out the book are Appendices containing detailed statistics, and multiple Indexes to help you navigate this comprehensive body of work.

A CLOSER LOOK AT WHAT'S INSIDE:

State of the Cannabis Industry 2019—A large, detailed section containing everything from the history of cannabis to current legal regulations. Objective reports on all aspects of the industry are also included, as are listings of Canadian and foreign trade shows and conferences.

Cannabis Industry Buyer's Guide—In-depth company listings covering all essential aspects of the industry. This is your go-to source for crucial contacts you need to expand your business, grow your network, or answer your research questions.

Associations—Everything from professional associations to health organizations, including international bodies essential to the industry.

Finance and Venture Capital—All the information you need on insurance, banking, and industry investment.

Law Firms—Find out which law firms offer services in the cannabis space, right down to specific lawyers' specialties!

Government—Federal and provincial departments and agencies that regulate and oversee the cannabis industry in Canada. This is your source for the best contacts in government.

Education—Colleges, universities and specialized schools that offer or are planning to offer cannabis-related courses.

Health—Locations of specialized health facilities, including mental health and addiction treatment programs across the country.

Publications—Listings of Canadian and foreign magazines, both in print and online, serving members of the cannabis community.

AVAILABLE ONLINE!

The *Canadian Cannabis Guide* is also available online on Canada's Information Resource Centre (CIRC). Thousands of companies and contacts are just a click away! Search by name or type of organization, subject, location, contact name or title and postal code. Export results and create mailing lists with this easy-to-use online database – an essential tool for researchers, students, marketing professionals and industry experts alike.

GREY HOUSE PUBLISHING CANADA

For more information please contact Grey House Publishing Canada
Tel.: (866)-433-4739 or (416) 644-6479 Fax: (416) 644-1904 | info@greyhouse.ca | www.greyhouse.ca

Cannabis au Canada

Cannabis du Canada est une ressource unique qui porte sur tous les aspects de cette industrie en pleine expansion. Il comprend des entrées exhaustives ainsi qu'une vaste gamme de rapports et de statistiques : vous y trouverez tout ce qu'il y a à savoir sur ce marché désormais légal, y compris des renseignements à portée internationale.

La première édition inclut le document l'État de l'industrie du cannabis 2019 sur l'histoire de la marijuana, les réglementations en vigueur ainsi que des rapports éclairants et des annonces de salons commerciaux et de congrès à venir.

Les lecteurs découvriront également le tout nouveau guide de l'acheteur de l'industrie du cannabis qui couvre un vaste éventail de sujets : des producteurs autorisés aux sociétés de conseil en passant par les sociétés de sécurité et plus encore. Toutes les entrées comprennent des champs spécialisés qui vont bien plus loin que le nom et l'adresse : elles regorgent de contacts essentiels et actuels.

PARMI LES RESSOURCES SUPPLÉMENTAIRES, MENTIONNONS :

- Associations de l'industrie
- Sociétés financières et de capital de risque
- Cabinets d'avocats
- Agences gouvernementales
- Établissements de soins de santé et de traitement
- Publications

Des annexes avec des statistiques détaillées et plusieurs index vous aident à parcourir cet ouvrage exhaustif.

UN EXAMEN PLUS APPROFONDI DU CONTENU :

L'état de l'industrie du cannabis en 2019—Une section détaillée volumineuse : de l'histoire du cannabis à la réglementation actuelle. S'y trouvent également des rapports objectifs portant sur tous les aspects de l'industrie, des entrées relatives aux salons professionnels ainsi qu'aux conférences, au Canada et à l'étranger.

Guide de l'acheteur—Industrie du cannabis : entrées commerciales exhaustives sur tous les aspects essentiels de l'industrie. Il constitue votre source d'information par excellence de personnes-ressources essentielles à l'expansion de votre entreprise et de votre réseau ou à la recherche de réponses.

Associations—Des associations professionnelles aux organismes de santé, y compris les organismes internationaux essentiels à l'industrie.

Finances et capital-risque—Toute l'information dont vous avez besoin au sujet de l'assurance, des services bancaires et du secteur des placements.

Cabinets d'avocats—Découvrez les cabinets d'avocats qui offrent des services reliés aux enjeux du cannabis, jusqu'aux domaines de spécialité d'avocats précis!

Gouvernement—Les agences et ministères fédéraux et provinciaux qui réglementent et surveillent l'industrie du cannabis au Canada. Cette source vous offre les meilleurs contacts à l'échelle du gouvernement.

Enseignement—Collèges, universités et écoles spécialisées qui offrent des cours ayant trait au cannabis ou qui comptent le futur.

Santé—L'emplacement d'établissements de santé spécialisés, notamment en santé mentale et en programmes de traitement des dépendances, partout au pays.

Publications—Listes de magazines, canadiens et étrangers, imprimés et en ligne, que peuvent consulter les participants du secteur du cannabis.

OFFERT EN LIGNE!

Le *Guide canadien du cannabis* sera également offert en ligne dans le Centre de documentation du Canada (CIRC). Un seul clic vous donne accès à des milliers d'entreprises et de personnes-ressources! Effectuez une recherche par nom ou par type d'organisation, par sujet, par emplacement, par code postal, par personne-ressource ou par titre. Exportez les résultats pour créer des listes d'envoi grâce à cette base de données en ligne conviviale, un outil essentiel tant pour les chercheurs, étudiants, professionnels du marketing que pour les experts de l'industrie.

GREY HOUSE PUBLISHING CANADA
Pour obtenir plus d'information, veuillez contacter Grey House Publishing Canada
par tél. : 1 866 433-4739 ou 416 644-6479 par téléc. : 416 644-1904 | info@greyhouse.ca | www.greyhouse.ca

Health Guide Canada
An Informative Handbook on Health Services in Canada

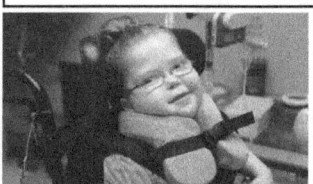

Health Guide Canada: An informative handbook on chronic and mental illnesses and health services in Canada offers a comprehensive overview of 107 chronic and mental illnesses, from Addison's to Wilson's disease. Each chapter includes an easy-to-understand medical description, plus a wide range of condition-specific support services and information resources that deal with the variety of issues concerning those with a chronic or mental illness, as well as those who support the illness community.

Health Guide Canada contains thousands of ways to deal with the many aspects of chronic or mental health disorder. It includes associations, government agencies, libraries and resource centres, educational facilities, hospitals and publications. In addition to chapters dealing with specific chronic or mental conditions, there is a chapter relevant to the health industry in general, as well as others dealing with charitable foundations, death and bereavement groups, homeopathic medicine, indigenous issues and sports for the disabled.

Specific sections include:

- Educational Material
- Section I: Chronic & Mental Illnesses
- Section II: General Resources
- Section III: Appendices
- Section IV: Statistics

Each listing will provide a description, address (including website, email address and social media links, if possible) and executives' names and titles, as well as a number of details specific to that type of organization.

In addition to patients and families, hospital and medical centre personnel can find the support they need in their work or study. *Health Guide Canada* is full of resources crucial for people with chronic illness as they transition from diagnosis to home, home to work, and work to community life.

PRINT OR ONLINE – QUICK AND EASY ACCESS TO ALL THE INFORMATION YOU NEED!

Available in softcover print or electronically via the web, *Health Guide Canada* provides instant access to the people you need and the facts you want every time. Whereas the print edition is verified and updated annually, ongoing changes are added to the web version on a regular basis. The web version allows you to narrow your search by using index fields such as name or type of organization, subject, location, contact name or title and postal code.

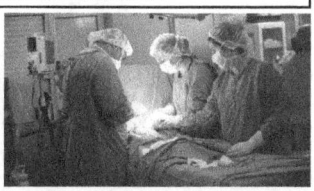

HEALTH GUIDE CANADA HELPS YOU FIND WHAT YOU NEED WITH THESE VALUABLE SOURCING TOOLS!

Entry Name Index—An alphabetical list of all entries, providing a quick and easy way to access any listing in this edition.

Tabs—Main sections are tabbed for easy look-up. Headers on each page make it easy to locate the data you need.

Create your own contact lists! Online subscribers have the option to instantly generate their own contact lists and export them into spreadsheets for further use—a great alternative to high cost list broker services.

GREY HOUSE PUBLISHING CANADA For more information please contact Grey House Publishing Canada
Tel.: (866)-433-4739 or (416) 644-6479 Fax: (416) 644-1904 | info@greyhouse.ca | www.greyhouse.ca

Guide canadien de la santé
Un manuel informatif au sujet des services en santé au Canada

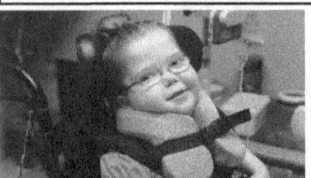

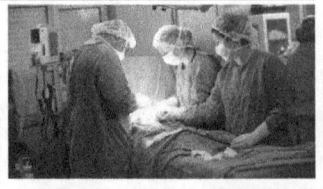

Le *Guide canadien de la santé : un manuel informatif au sujet des maladies chroniques et mentales de même que des services en santé au Canada* donne un aperçu exhaustif de 107 maladies chroniques et mentales, de la maladie d'Addison à celle de Wilson. Chaque chapitre comprend une description médicale facile à comprendre, une vaste gamme de services de soutien particuliers à l'état et des ressources documentaires qui portent sur diverses questions relatives aux personnes qui sont aux prises avec une maladie chronique ou mentale et à ceux qui soutiennent la communauté liée à cette maladie.

Le *Guide canadien de la santé* contient des milliers de moyens pour composer avec divers aspects d'une maladie chronique ou d'un problème de santé mentale. Il comprend des associations, des organismes gouvernementaux, des bibliothèques et des centres de documentation, des services d'éducation, des hôpitaux et des publications. En plus des chapitres qui portent sur des états chroniques ou mentaux, un chapitre traite de l'industrie de la santé en général; d'autres abordent les fondations qui réalisent des rêves, les groupes de soutien axés sur le décès et le deuil, la médecine homéopathique, les questions autochtones et les sports pour les personnes handicapées. Les sections incluent

- Matériel didactique
- Section I : Les maladies chroniques ou mentales
- Section II : Les ressources génériques
- Section III : Les annexes
- Section IV : Les statistiques

Chaque entrée comprend une description, une adresse (y compris le site Web, le courriel et les liens des médias sociaux, lorsque possible), les noms et titres des directeurs de même que plusieurs détails particuliers à ce type d'organisme.

Les membres du personnel des hôpitaux et des centres médicaux peuvent trouver, au même titre que parents et familles, le soutien dont ils ont besoin dans le cadre de leur travail ou de leurs études. Le *Guide canadien de la santé* est rempli de ressources capitales pour les personnes qui souffrent d'une maladie chronique alors qu'elles passent du diagnostic au retour à la maison, de la maison au travail et du travail à la vie au sein de la communauté.

OFFERT EN FORMAT PAPIER OU EN LIGNE—UN ACCÈS RAPIDE ET FACILE À TOUS LES RENSEIGNEMENTS DONT VOUS AVEZ BESOIN!

Offert sous couverture souple ou en format électronique grâce au web, le *Guide canadien de la santé* donne invariablement un accès instantané aux personnes et aux faits dont vous avez besoin. Si la version imprimée est vérifiée et mise à jour annuellement, des changements continus sont apportés mensuellement à la base de données en ligne. Servez-vous de la version en ligne afin de circonscrire vos recherches grâce à des champs spéciaux de l'index comme le nom de l'organisation ou son type, le sujet, l'emplacement, le nom de la personne-ressource ou son titre et le code postal.

LE GUIDE CANADIEN DE LA SANTÉ VOUS AIDERA À TROUVER CE DONT VOUS AVEZ BESOIN GRÂCE À CES OUTILS DE REPÉRAGE PRÉCIEUX!

Répertoire nominatif—une list alphabétique offrant un moyen rapide et facile d'accéder à toute liste de cette édition.

Onglets—les sections principals possèdent un onglet pour une consultation facile. Les notes en tête de chaque page vous aident à trouver les données voulues.

Créez vos propres listes! Les abonnés au service en ligne peuvent générer instantanément leurs propres listes de contacts et les exporter en format feuille de calcul pour une utilisation approfondie – une solution de rechange géniale aux services dispendieux d'un commissionnaire en publipostage.

GREY HOUSE PUBLISHING CANADA

Pour obtenir plus d'information, veuillez contacter Grey House Publishing Canada
par tél. : 1 866 433-4739 ou 416 644-6479 par téléc. : 416 644-1904 | info@greyhouse.ca | www.greyhouse.ca

THE FACTS FOUND FAST!

Tap into FP Corporate Surveys and access all the facts and figures you need to make better informed decisions.

Covering over 6,300 publicly traded Canadian companies, FP Survey - Industrials and FP Survey - Mines & Energy are loaded with financial and operational information. Discover companies' financial results, capital and debt structure, key corporate developments, major shareholders, directors and executive officers, subsidiaries and more!

The ideal complement, FP Survey - Predecessor & Defunct, provides a comprehensive record of changes to Canadian public corporations dating back almost 90 years.

FP Corporate Surveys are completely unbiased, current and credible - make your investment decisions based on the facts.

ALL THE IN-DEPTH INFORMATION THAT YOU NEED – ALL IN ONE PLACE

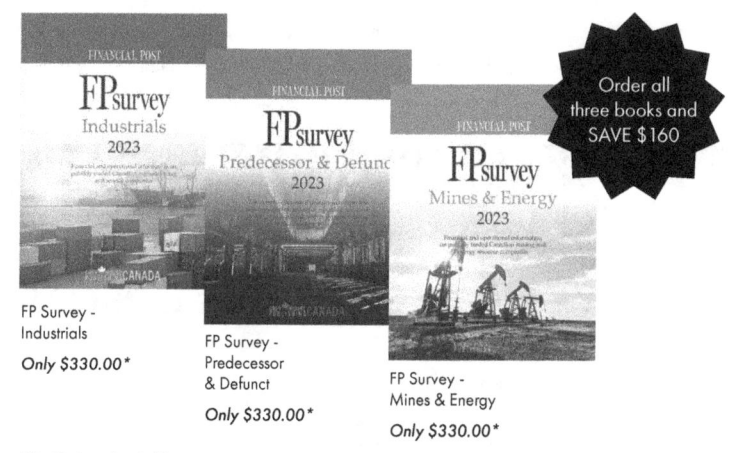

Order all three books and SAVE $160

FP Survey - Industrials
Only $330.00*

FP Survey - Predecessor & Defunct
Only $330.00*

FP Survey - Mines & Energy
Only $330.00*

*Plus shipping and applicable taxes

3 Easy Ways to Order

Phone: 1.866.433.4739 • Fax: 416.644.1904 • Email: info@greyhouse.ca

GREY HOUSE PUBLISHING CANADA

To Order: Toll Free Tel 1.866.433.4739 • Fax 416.644.1904

Financial Post Fixed Income Books are owned by Financial Post Data, a division of Postmedia Network Inc., and are exclusively printed and distributed by Grey House Publishing Canada.

Make Smarter Investment Decisions

FP Advisor

The ultimate online investment and research tool

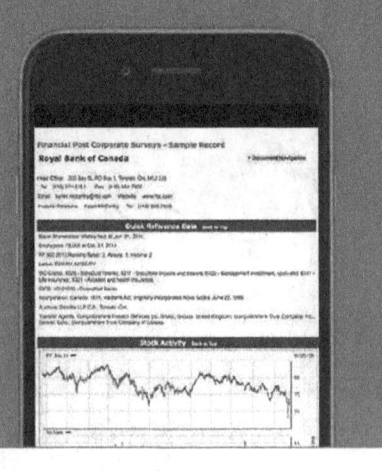

As the most trusted and reliable source of corporate data, FP Advisor provides detailed information about public and private companies across Canada, archival financial data, useful analytical and lead generation tools, and more—all in one convenient place.

FP Advisor includes:

- Corporate Snapshots
- Corporate Surveys
- Corporate Analyzer
- Investor Reports
- Historical Reports
- Industry Reports
- Predecessor & Defunct
- Mergers & Acquisition
- Dividends
- New Issues
- Fixed Income
- Directory of Directors

" FP Advisor is a very important source of information for us. We rely extensively on Predecessor & Defunct and Mergers & Acquisitions to track companies over time. Historical Reports include valuable current operations and ownership details that can be difficult to find elsewhere."
Kathy West, Head, Winspear Business Library, University of Alberta

Get a free trial today!

fpadvisor@postmedia.com | legacy-fpadvisor.financialpost.com

POSTMEDIA

//FINANCIAL POST

FPbonds
Government

Additional Publications
For more detailed information or to place an order, see the back of the book.

CANADIAN ALMANAC & DIRECTORY 2024
Répetoire et almanach canadien
2,367 pages, 8 ½ x 11, Hardcover
177th edition, December 2023
ISBN 978-1-63700-702-0
ISSN 0068-8193
A combination of textual material, charts, colour photographs and directory listings, the *Canadian Almanac & Directory* provides the most comprehensive picture of Canada, from physical attributes to economic and business summaries to leisure and recreation.

CANADIAN WHO'S WHO 2024
1,200 pages, 8 3/8 x 10 7/8, Hardcover
December 2023
ISBN 978-1-63700-704-4
ISSN 0068-9963
Published for over 100 years, this authoritative annual publication offers access to the top 10,000 notable Canadians in all walks of life, including details such as date and place of birth, education, family details, career information, memberships, creative works, honours, languages, and awards, together with full addresses. Included are outstanding Canadians from business, academia, politics, sports, the arts and sciences, and more, selected because of the positions they hold in Canadian society, or because of the contributions they have made to Canada.

FINANCIAL POST DIRECTORY OF DIRECTORS 2024
Répertoire des administrateurs
1,759 pages, 5 7/8 x 9, Hardcover
77th edition, September 2023
ISBN 978-1-63700-700-6
ISSN 0071-5042
Published biennially and annually since 1931, this comprehensive resource offers readers access to approximately 16,900 executive contacts from Canada's top 1,400 corporations. The directory provides a definitive list of directorships and offices held by noteworthy Canadian business people, as well as details on prominent Canadian companies (both public and private), including company name, contact information and the names of executive officers and directors. Includes all-new front matter and three indexes.

MAJOR CANADIAN CITIES: COMPARED & RANKED
Comparaison et classement des principales villes canadiennes
1,372 pages, 8 ½ x 11, Softcover
2nd edition, January 2024
ISBN 978-8-89179-049-0
This second edition of *Major Canadian Cities: Compared and Ranked* has been completely revised with 2021 census data, including new tables and a refreshed layout. It provides an in-depth comparison and analysis of the 50 most populated cities in Canada. Each chapter incorporates information from dozens of resources to create the following major sections: Background, Study Rankings, and Statistical Tables.

CANADIAN PARLIAMENTARY GUIDE 2024
Guide parlementaire canadien
1,334 pages, 6 x 9, Hardcover
158th edition, March 2024
ISBN 978-1-63700-918-5
ISSN 0315-6168
Published annually since before Confederation, this indispensable guide to government in Canada provides information on federal and provincial governments, with biographical sketches of government members, descriptions of government institutions, and historical text and charts. With significant bilingual sections, the Guide covers elections from Confederation to the present, including the most recent provincial elections.

ASSOCIATIONS CANADA 2024
Associations du Canada
2,144 pages, 8 ½ x 11, Softcover
45th edition, February 2024
ISBN 978-1-63700-916-1
ISSN 1484-2408
Over 20,000 entries profile Canadian and international organizations active in Canada. Over 2,000 subject classifications index activities, professions and interests served by associations. Includes listings of NGOs, institutes, coalitions, social agencies, federations, foundations, trade unions, fraternal orders, and political parties. Fully indexed by subject, acronym, budget, conference, executive name, geographic location, mailing list availability, and registered charitable organization.

FINANCIAL SERVICES CANADA 2023-2024
Services financiers au Canada
1,516 pages, 8 ½ x 11, Softcover
25th edition, May 2023
ISBN 978-1-63700-692-4
ISSN 1484-2408
This directory of Canadian financial institutions and organizations includes banks and depository institutions, non-depository institutions, investment management firms, financial planners, insurance companies, accountants, major law firms, associations, and financial technology companies. Fully indexed.

LIBRARIES CANADA 2023-2024
Bibliothèques Canada
900 pages, 8 ½ x 11, Softcover
37th edition, July 2023
ISBN 978-1-67300-690-0
ISSN 1920-2849
Libraries Canada offers comprehensive information on Canadian libraries, resource centres, business information centres, professional associations, regional library systems, archives, library schools, government libraries, and library technical programs.

CAREERS & EMPLOYMENT CANADA 2021
Carrières et emploi Canada
970 pages, 8 ½ x 11, Softcover
1st edition, October 2020
ISBN 978-1-61925-713-5
Careers & Employment Canada is a go-to resource for job-seekers across Canada, with detailed, current information on everything from industry associations to summer job opportunities. Divided into five helpful sections, plus three indexes, this guide contains 10,000 organizations and 20,000 industry contacts to aid in research and jump-start careers in a variety of fields.